HUTCHINSON POCKET

Quiz Book

Other titles in the Hutchinson Pocket series:

HUTCHINSON POCKET

Quiz Book

Questions compiled by
Hilary Murphy

Helicon

Copyright © Helicon Publishing Ltd 1993

Helicon Publishing Ltd
42 Hythe Bridge Street
Oxford OX1 2EP

Printed and bound in Great Britain by
Unwin Brothers Ltd, Old Woking, Surrey

ISBN 0 09 178101 9

British Cataloguing in Publication Data

A catalogue record for this book is available
from the British Library

Editorial director
Michael Upshall

Project editor
Hilary McGlynn

Text editor
Louise Jones

Page make-up
Helen Bird

Production
Tony Ballsdon

Contents

Numbers are quiz numbers, not page numbers

Foreword

This book contains 100 quizzes graded into three sections, according to level of difficulty, and grouped into 28 different categories. The quizzes are aimed mainly at adults, but some questions in the first section, at least, should be answerable by children from the age of about 12.

Answers are at the end of the book; the page number of the appropriate answer section is given at the end of each quiz. After each answer, in brackets, is a reference to the relevant entry or entries in *The Hutchinson Encyclopedia, 10th edition*. By using the system of cross-references within the *Encyclopedia*, – the source for all these questions – readers can further explore questions of particular interest.

EASY

★

1   What sort of woollen headgear was named after a battle of the Crimean War?

2   Which year (in figures) is displayed by the seven Roman numerals listed in descending order?

3   Whose tomb is situated in Arlington Cemetery, Washington, at the Arc de Triomphe, Paris, and in Westminster Abbey, London?

4   What is the surname of the Hungarian inventor whose multicoloured, rotatable cube became a world cult?

5   What is the set of 26 letters whose name is derived from the names of two Greek letters?

6   How long is the appointed term of office of the secretary general of the United Nations?

7   What is the name common to three Scottish kings, eight popes and three tsars of Russia?

8   Who was elected the first black Anglican archbishop of Cape Town in 1988?

9   What is thrown backhand by the people who contest the championships of the World Flying Disc Association held in the USA?

10 What were first issued in 1950 and allowed people to 'pay by plastic'?

(See p. 111 for answers)

1   What once covered 14% of the Earth's land area, but by 1991 over half had been destroyed?

2   Which country produces the world's largest quantity of municipal waste per person per year at over five-sixths of a ton?

3   What was the original name of the British Green Party when it was formed in 1973?

4   What is the collective term for substances such as coal, oil and natural gas, the burning of which produces carbon dioxide?

5   Which environmental pressure group was founded in the UK in 1971?

6   What describes all the species protected by the CITES Agreement?

7   What contributes to the greenhouse effect at lower atmospheric levels, but in the upper atmosphere protects life on Earth?

8   Which Ukrainian town's nuclear power station exploded in 1986, causing contamination as far away as Sweden and the UK?

9   What is the name for land in Britain officially designated 'not to be built on but to be preserved as open space'?

10   What is dispensed from the green pump, and must be used if a car has a catalytic converter?

(See p. 111 for answers)

True or False?

1 Tomatoes and potatoes grow on plants belonging to the same family as deadly nightshade. True or false?

2 Jazz musician William Basie was better known as Duke. True or false?

3 Nicotine, in its pure form, is one of the most powerful poisons known. True or false?

4 Antarctica has less annual precipitation than the Sahara desert. True or false?

5 The Duke of Edinburgh's grandfather was King George I of Greece. True or false?

6 Prince is the real first name of Prince, the US pop star. True or false?

7 Anchorage is the capital of Alaska. True or false?

8 All century years such as 1700, 1800 and 1900 are leap years because they divide by four. True or false?

9 Caligula, the Roman emperor, gave a consulship to his horse, Incitatus. True or false?

10 All four feet of a beaver are webbed. True or false?

(See p. 112 for answers)

Sport 4

1   Which stroke is totally disallowed in table tennis but must be every stroke in badminton?

2   Where would you see the events of calf roping, bull riding, steer wrestling and bronco busting contested?

3   In 1985 who, at the age of 17, became the youngest winner of a Wimbledon singles title?

4   Which world champion heavyweight boxer's middle name was originally Marcellus?

5   What is the third ball to be potted in the sequence of colours in snooker?

6   What is a version of the Gaelic word for 'pole' indicating an object tossed in the Highland Games?

7   Which equestrian sport tests the all-round ability of the horse and rider?

8   What is an alternative name for the sport of free falling?

9   Which city played host to the 1992 Summer Olympics?

10 Which swimming stroke propels the body through the water at the greatest speed?

(See p. 112 for answers)

Geography 5

1   Three-quarters of which continent lie within the tropics?

2   Which European capital was originally two places, separated by the River Danube, whose names have been joined to form the city's name?

3   Which weather system often results in clear, hot, sunny days in summer and fine, frosty days in winter?

4   Which river's waters, headwaters and tributaries drain half the continent of South America?

5   The equator passes through many countries; which one bears its Spanish name?

6   What is the name of the river of which the Niagara Falls are a part?

7   Which country is the second largest in the world, in area?

8   Of which European country do the Magyars make up 92% of the population?

9   Which is the largest city in the largest state of the USA?

10   Which is the only parallel to divide the Earth into hemispheres?

(See p. 113 for answers)

Choices

1   The colour of a polar bear's skin is: a) black b) pink
    c) white

2   Mother Teresa of Calcutta was born in: a) Afghanistan
    b) Albania c) India

3   In 1721 Britain's first prime minister took office. How
    many since then have been Labour prime ministers? a) 6
    b) 8 c) 10

4   What did the USA buy from the Russians for $72 million?
    a) The rights to the film of Lenin's life story
    b) Tchaikovsky's original manuscripts c) Alaska

5   The capybara is a South American rodent whose average
    weight is: a) 8 oz b) 8 lb c) 8 stone

6   The part of a sundial which casts a shadow to tell the time
    is called: a) an elfon b) a gnomon c) a pixion

7   The ice in the Antarctic reaches a depth of: a) 16 ft
    b) 1,600 ft c) 16,000 ft

8   In 1953 Winston Churchill won a Nobel prize for: a) Peace
    b) Literature c) Economics

9   The basic currency unit of Vietnam is: a) the ding b) the
    deng c) the dong

10 Nelson lost an eye in 1794 and an arm in 1797; they were
    his: a) right arm/right eye b) right arm/left eye c) right eye/
    left arm

(See p. 113 for answers)

History 7

1   What were the names of the royal first cousins who married in 1840 and had four sons and five daughters?

2   What was built from the Tyne to the Solway in AD 122 –6 as the northern border of Roman Britain?

3   Name the 11th-century survey documented in two volumes and kept in London's Public Record Office.

4   What did Pope Pius V do to Elizabeth I and Pope Paul III do to Henry VIII?

5   What killed 100,000 of London's 400,000 population in 1665?

6   Whose exploration of the New World had its quincentenary in 1992?

7   Which two countries were joined in the Act of Union 1707?

8   Which war was fought over 'the Union' and the emancipation of slaves?

9   What was the name of the flag captain who attended mortally wounded Nelson at the Battle of Trafalgar?

10   Which war made Florence Nightingale famous?

(See p. 114 for answers)

1 Which flightless marine birds of the southern hemisphere live in rookeries?

2 What is the larva of a toad called?

3 Which bird feeds with its head upside-down and its beak held horizontally beneath the water?

4 Of which reptile are there only two species, one living in the Mississippi and the other in China?

5 Which birds of prey have acute hearing, binocular vision and heads which can turn 180°?

6 Which species of decapod has varieties called 'fiddler', 'spider' and 'hermit'?

7 Which is the largest animal ever to exist on Earth, whose food is the tiny shrimp-like krill?

8 Which microscopic organisms form the basis of marine and freshwater food chains?

9 Which bird, a member of the cuckoo family, is often seen dashing along the highways of the southern USA and Mexico ... hence its name?

10 What is the name of the seasonal journey undertaken by many animals to distant feeding and breeding grounds?

(See p. 114 for answers)

1 Who said 'That's one small step for a man, one giant leap for mankind' on 20 July 1969?

2 Which town in Umbria was the birthplace of St Francis?

3 What is the term for a person with assets of over 1,000 million dollars?

4 Who was the Roman Catholic convert arrested on 4 November 1605 in the cellars of the Houses of Parliament?

5 Which school near Elgin was attended by the Duke of Edinburgh and Prince Charles?

6 Carlo Collodi wrote a story about a wooden puppet which became human. What is its title?

7 For which group of people is Romany the native language?

8 What is the acronym for the agency set up in 1923 to provide co-operation between police forces worldwide?

9 Which public official can order an inquest into instances of sudden, violent or suspicious death?

10 What is the Latin word for 'elsewhere' which we use to mean that the person under suspicion was somewhere else when the crime was committed?

(See p. 115 for answers)

1   Of the four American states whose names begin with 'A', which ends in a different letter?

2   What was the name and rank of Stormin' Norman, the supreme commander of the Allied Forces during the Gulf War?

3   What is the written statute containing all the fundamental laws of the USA?

4   Which boxer was stripped of his world heavyweight title for refusing to be drafted into the army in 1968?

5   Which film actress, originally called Frances Gumm, had the theme song 'Over the Rainbow'?

6   For what are the cities Reno, Atlantic City and Las Vegas renowned?

7   Which American film actor was governor of California from 1966–74?

8   If all the US states were listed in alphabetical order, which would be last?

9   Which bandleader led the US Army Air Force Band in Europe and composed his own signature tune 'Moonlight Serenade'?

10   In which city is Graceland, Elvis Presley's home?

(See p. 115 for answers)

1   Which British resort is famous for its tower and its illuminations?

2   Which English county was created in 1974 when Bristol was merged with parts of south Gloucestershire and north Somerset?

3   Which wooded area of Nottinghamshire was once a royal park and hunting ground?

4   In which county are England's largest lake and highest mountain situated?

5   Which district of London gave its name to the Prime Meridian?

6   Which motorway, the first in the UK, was opened as the Preston Bypass in 1958?

7   Where in the British Isles are Macgillycuddy's Reeks and the Giant's Causeway?

8   Which of the countries in the British Isles is said to have the highest density of sheep in the world?

9   Which mountain system is sometimes referred to as 'the backbone of England'?

10 What is the name of the winter sports centre in the Cairngorms?

(See p. 116 for answers)

1   What is the title shared by four books of the New Testament?

2   Who was the brother of Martha, raised from the dead by Jesus?

3   Who made the Golden Calf for the Hebrews to worship while Moses was on Mount Sinai?

4   Which book of the New Testament describes the Last Judgement and the end of the world?

5   Which book of the Old Testament is a collection of moral and ethical maxims?

6   Which book of the Bible contains the story of the Great Flood?

7   Which was the Canaanite town whose walls fell at the blast of Joshua's trumpets?

8   Who committed suicide after receiving 30 pieces of silver as payment for betraying his master?

9   What are the 150 sacred poems and songs of praise said to have been written by David?

10   Who was formed from the dust by God, then given the breath of life, to become the progenitor of the human race?

(See p. 116 for answers)

1   Who was noted for his cameo walk-ons in his own films?

2   What was Arnold Schwarzenegger's original nationality?

3   Which American film director is associated with Jaws, ET, and Indiana Jones?

4   Which actor won Oscars for his performances in *Kramer vs. Kramer* and *Rain Man*?

5   Who was the cartoon character married to Jessica in a film starring Bob Hoskins?

6   Who was the hero of the books by Ian Fleming which, when made into films, made Sean Connery and Roger Moore international stars?

7   What was the surname shared by the actresses who starred in *My Fair Lady* and *The African Queen*?

8   Why did *The Jazz Singer*, starring Al Jolson, make history in 1927?

9   Which film actor shot to fame in 1976 with his portrayal of the boxer Rocky Balboa?

10 Which film, released by the Disney studios in 1938, was the first feature-length animated film?

(See p. 117 for answers)

Literature 14

1   What is the title of the Herman Melville novel whose alternative title is *The Whale*?

2   Which author created the sleuths Miss Jane Marple and Hercule Poirot?

3   Who was the author of *The Wind in the Willows*, dramatized by A A Milne as *Toad of Toad Hall*?

4   Who is the narrator of Arthur Conan Doyle's Sherlock Holmes stories?

5   What was the pen-name of the Mississippi river boat pilot who created the fictional characters of Tom Sawyer and Huckleberry Finn?

6   What is the name of Don Quixote's servant in the novel by Cervantes?

7   Which of Tolkien's fantasy characters inhabit the world of Middle Earth?

8   Which literary family lived at the parsonage in the village of Haworth on the Yorkshire Moors?

9   Which English author, who sometimes wrote under the name 'Boz', portrayed the social and economic ills of Victorian England in his novels?

10 Which fictional character is said to be based on Vlad the Impaler, a Transylvanian king of Wallachia?

(See p. 117 for answers)

True or False?

1. The legendary female warriors called Amazons lived in the Amazon basin. True or false?

2. The word 'dinosaur' is derived from the Greek for 'terrible lizard'. True or false?

3. Richard the Lionheart spent all but six months of his ten-year reign in England. True or false?

4. Contestants in the Olympic Games of ancient Greece competed naked. True or false?

5. The American CIA is the equivalent organization of Britain's CID. True or false?

6. Titus and Philemon are two books of the New Testament. True or false?

7. Big Ben is the clock in the tower of the Houses of Parliament. True or false?

8. In computing, a kilobyte is 1,000 bytes. True or false?

9. The dogfish is actually a small shark. True or false?

10. The dingo, Australia's wild dog, cannot bark. True or false?

(See p. 118 for answers)

1   What, specifically, are the metals amalgam, solder, pewter and steel?

2   Which branch of science has four fundamental principles: addition, subtraction, multiplication and division?

3   What is the name given to the longest side of a right-angled triangle?

4   What is the name of the technique used to produce three-dimensional pictures by means of laser light?

5   In which area of science are the terms CPU, PC and VDU used?

6   What, in genetics, is the term denoting the transmission of traits and characteristics from parents to offspring?

7   What are classified by their measurement in degrees as 'right', 'reflex', 'obtuse' or 'acute'?

8   What is the most abundant element in the universe?

9   What was the commodity that made Alfred Nobel's fortune, used to fund the Nobel prizes?

10   What is the generic term for the mechanical, electrical and electronic components of a computer?

(See p. 118 for answers)

Food and Drink 17

1   What is the name for the enhancers, emulsifiers, colourings and flavourings used in foods, usually given E-numbers in Europe?

2   Which town in southwest France is the centre of a wine-growing district famous for its brandy?

3   What is made from chicle, the milky-white fluid made into a popular American confection?

4   Which fish native to the Caspian Sea, sometimes called a beluga, is the source of the highest quality caviar?

5   What is another name for the dietary fibre which provides food bulk to aid digestion?

6   Which traditional dish is made from a sheep's heart, liver and lungs, minced with oatmeal and seasoning, and boiled in the sheep's stomach?

7   What is the purple fruit of the eggplant which is used as a vegetable?

8   Which tree of the laurel family produces a pear-shaped fruit used as a vegetable and usually eaten raw?

9   Which young French wine is released annually on the third Thursday in November?

10 What is eaten traditionally in the UK on the day before Ash Wednesday?

(See p. 119 for answers)

Theatre and Entertainment 18

1   Which of Bob Kane's strip-cartoon characters has the secret identity of millionaire playboy Bruce Wayne?

2   What is the pen-name of James Wight, whose books about his experiences as a Yorkshire vet were made into several television series?

3   Which Australian created Barry Mackenzie for *Private Eye* and Dame Edna Everage for stage and television?

4   Which form of traditional Christmas entertainment has the hero played by a woman, and a female character played by a man?

5   Which type of music developed from the spirituals sung in the Baptist churches of the southern USA?

6   Who are the two characters, a dim-witted socialite and his urbane manservant, created by P G Wodehouse?

7   Which British-born actress played the original Eliza Doolittle on the London stage in 1956?

8   Which writer of children's books also wrote *Tales of the Unexpected* for television and the screenplay for the film *You Only Live Twice*?

9   Which group of Jim Henson puppets first appeared on American television in *Sesame Street*?

10   What is the title of the Andrew Lloyd Webber musical based on a collection of animal poems by T S Eliot?

(See p. 119 for answers)

Chemistry

1   What is the name of the dye which turns red on contact with acid and blue with alkali?

2   Which gas, produced by rotting vegetation, causes the phenomenon known as will o' the wisp?

3   What has the chemical symbol C_2H_5OH and is the intoxicating part of a drink?

4   What are the three states of matter?

5   Which common mineral is used to make casts, moulds, blackboard chalk and plaster of Paris?

6   Which process causes bread to rise and produces bubbles in beer?

7   Which element is used as a disinfectant, as a bleaching agent and to purify water?

8   What is the mixture of potassium nitrate, charcoal and sulphur which constitutes the explosive used in fireworks?

9   What is a very hard, transparent form of carbon, whose crystals are octahedral in shape?

10 What is the common name for sodium chloride?

(See p. 120 for answers)

1   Which teeth are the third molars, and are always the last to erupt?

2   What is the average human body temperature when taken by a thermometer under the tongue?

3   What beats more than 2,000 million times during an average lifetime – or about 72 beats per minute?

4   What is secreted by the pancreas to regulate blood sugar levels?

5   What are the two main veins in the neck, returning blood from the brain to the heart?

6   Which parts of the body are formed by the bones of the metatarsals and phalanges?

7   Where in the body are the cerebellum, the medulla and the hypothalamus?

8   What is the term for a series of uncontrollable intakes of air caused by sudden spasms of the diaphragm?

9   What are the very narrow blood vessels which form a network between arteries and veins?

10   What makes up 60–70% of human body weight?

(See p. 120 for answers)

1   Which 18th-century cattle-thief, smuggler, robber and highwayman was hanged at York in 1739?

2   What is the term used to denote the unauthorized and illegal accessing of computer programs, often with criminal intent?

3   What does the 'MI' of MI5 and MI6 stand for?

4   What was the term popularized by Winston Churchill for the imaginary boundary dividing Europe between the capitalist West and the communist East?

5   On which spring day is a hoax victim referred to as a 'gowk' in Scotland and a *poisson d'avril* in France?

6   Which nomadic people have an Arabic name which means 'desert-dweller'?

7   Where were Anne Boleyn, Catherine Howard and Lady Jane Grey beheaded?

8   What was the surname of Charles, the dog expert, who organized his first dog show in 1886?

9   What goes after 'People's', 'Atlantic' and 'Citizen's' for three documents drawn up in 1837, 1941 and 1991 respectively?

10 What is the unit used for measuring the fineness of yarn, especially in stockings and tights?

(See p. 121 for answers)

1   Who was the youngest-ever leader of the Labour Party, elected in 1983?

2   Which is the lower house of the British parliament?

3   Who was the last foreign secretary to serve in Margaret Thatcher's cabinet, an MP who also contested the leadership after her resignation?

4   What is the name for the group of opposition spokesmen and spokeswomen who comment on the policies of government ministers?

5   In which parliament has the UK 81 seats for members who are elected for a five-year term?

6   Which British prime minister was succeeded by Mrs Thatcher?

7   Which publication documents all proceedings of the British parliament?

8   Which party leader was a Royal Marine and commando?

9   How many readings does an act of Parliament have in the House of Commons before being given royal assent?

10 What was the British government forced to abolish in 1991, replacing it with the council tax?

(See p. 121 for answers)

Mythology 23

1   Where was the legendary seat of King Arthur?

2   What did Daedalus construct for King Minos so that he could keep the Minotaur there?

3   Who was the ancient Egyptian redeemer god, husband of Isis?

4   What is the collective name for the three sisters who had wings, talons, huge teeth and snakes for hair?

5   Which king of Phrygia had his 'golden' wish granted?

6   Who spurned Echo's love and was punished by being made to fall in love with his own reflection?

7   Which mountain in Thessaly did the ancient Greeks believe to be home of the gods?

8   Where did Odin feast with the souls of dead heroes?

9   What sort of mythical creature is identified with the constellation Sagittarius?

10 Who left Ithaca on a ten-year voyage, leaving behind his wife Penelope and son Telemachus?

(See p. 122 for answers)

1   Which instrument's name translates literally as 'soft loud'?

2   What are performed at La Scala, Milan and at the auditorium in Covent Garden, London?

3   What is the name for the annual summer series of concerts held at the Royal Albert Hall, London, in which the audience originally walked about?

4   What were the surnames of Thomas and Arthur who collaborated to write 'The Savoy Operas'?

5   What was the nationality of Bartok, Kodaly and Liszt?

6   Which instrument is a pocket-sized reed-organ invented by Charles Wheatstone in 1829?

7   Why didn't Gustav Holst include Pluto in his 1918 orchestral suite *The Planets*?

8   Which instrument has 47 strings and seven pedals, and was introduced into the orchestra in the 19th century?

9   Which composer wrote 27 piano concertos, 23 string quartets, 35 violin sonatas and more than 50 symphonies?

10   Which instrument is a keyboard reed-organ, powered by foot pedals and used in American churches during the 1800s?

(See p. 122 for answers)

1   Which Apollo space mission was the first to land man on the Moon?

2   What was located in the Atlantic in 1987, 75 years after sinking off the Grand Banks southeast of Newfoundland?

3   Which airliner came into service in 1976, cutting the transatlantic crossing to less than three hours?

4   What do the initials HGV stand for?

5   What is London's equivalent of Moscow's Metro and New York's subway?

6   What word describes every space flight before the one undertaken by Yuri Gagarin in 1961?

7   What achieves lift-off and propulsion by means of a rotary wing?

8   What type of transport are ICEs, TGVs and HSTs?

9   What is the popular name for the Boeing 747?

10 What do we call a lightweight motorcycle with auxiliary pedal power?

(See p. 123 for answers)

1   Gargoyles were often carved on Gothic churches as:
a) frighteners to ward off the devil b) carvings done by
apprentices to achieve skill c) embellished waterspouts

2   Queen Victoria belonged to the royal house of: a) Windsor
b) Hanover c) Saxe-Coburg-Gotha

3   Was the mythical centaur: a) half-man/half-bull b) half-
man/half-horse c) half-man/half-goat?

4   No place in the UK is further from the sea than: a) $53^1/_2$
miles b) $74^1/_2$ miles c) $91^1/_2$ miles

5   Terry Waite's ordeal as a hostage in Lebanon lasted: a) 63
days b) 763 days c) 1,763 days

6   The president's wife who was the subject of a successful
musical written in 1978 was: a) Imelda Marcos b) Eva
Peron c) Jacqueline Kennedy

7   Which US writer moved to Europe, and took British
citizenship the year before he died? a) Henry James
b) T S Eliot c) W H Auden

8   The Great White Shark is the nickname of the golfer: a)
Jack Nicklaus b) Arnold Palmer c) Greg Norman

9   The approximate number of copies of Michael Jackson's
best-selling album *Thriller* sold worldwide was: a) 20
million b) 40 million c) 60 million

10 The average adult human digestive tract measures: a) 30 in
b) 30 ft c) 30 yd

(See p. 123 for answers)

1 In which religion do men take the last name 'Singh' and women 'Kaur'?

2 What, in the Christian church, occurs 49 days before Whit Sunday and 40 days after Shrove Tuesday?

3 In which religion must adherents visit Mecca at least once in a lifetime?

4 The followers of which religion observe the Sabbath from sunset on Friday to sunset on Saturday?

5 Which religion, established in India about 500 BC, has followers who strive for enlightenment?

6 Which members of the Christian Church believe that Christ will make a second appearance on Earth?

7 In which religion are the gods Brahma, Vishnu and Siva worshipped?

8 What is the name of the established Church of Scotland which follows a Calvinistic doctrine?

9 The members of which Christian sect have no ministers or priests, and gather for worship in a Meeting House?

10 In Buddhism, what is the name for the attainment of perfect serenity, achieved when all desires are eradicated?

(See p. 124 for answers)

1 In which Italian town was the artist Leonardo born?

2 Who designed the largest Protestant church in England, St Paul's Cathedral?

3 Which titled Yorkshire sculptor, known for his reclining figures, was an official war artist in World War II?

4 Which French post-Impressionist artist spent eight years of his life painting in Tahiti?

5 Which animals, sculpted by Edward Landseer, stand at the four corners of Trafalgar Square?

6 In front of which French art gallery is there a large glass pyramid designed by I M Pei?

7 Which 16th-century Belgian artist painted scenes of peasant life?

8 Which style of architecture was used in England during the 11th and 12th centuries?

9 Which modern building in Sydney was designed by Joern Utzon?

10 Which English artist was famous for his industrial Lancashire townscapes filled with matchstick figures?

(See p. 124 for answers)

1   What stands 1,050 ft tall in the Champ de Mars and was designed for the 1889 Paris Exhibition?

2   What is printed on most articles for sale and is read by a scanning device to identify the manufacturer and the product?

3   What has three main and seven foundation subjects and is followed in all UK primary and secondary schools?

4   Which Italian city was buried, along with Herculaneum, when Vesuvius erupted in AD 79?

5   Which European country is also known as the Hellenic Republic?

6   What was the dukedom bestowed on Philip Mountbatten on 19 November 1947, the day before his wedding?

7   What was abolished in Britain in 1965 for all crimes except treason?

8   Which emergency device was first used in 1945 and has since saved the lives of more than 5,000 pilots?

9   What is the official monetary unit of the European Community?

10 The Little Mermaid, a statue at the entrance to Copenhagen harbour, is a fairy-tale character created by which writer?

(See p. 125 for answers)

1   The discovery of which law provoked the surprised cry 'Eureka!'?

2   What is the unit for measuring the intensity of sound, often abbreviated to dB?

3   What was the name of the Polish-born scientist who died from the effects of the radiation she was studying?

4   Which Swedish scientist had a temperature scale named after him?

5   Which electronic device magnifies the strength of a signal?

6   What diverges rays of light, if it is concave?

7   What is any material that allows the passage of electricity and heat called?

8   How many colours are there in the spectrum when white light is separated?

9   What was the name of the unit of heat now replaced by the joule?

10   What is the term used to denote the tendency of an object to remain in a state of rest until acted upon by an external force?

(See p. 125 for answers)

1. Which popular singer was born in Tupelo, Mississippi, and died in Memphis, Tennessee?

2. What is the stage name of the rock singer Reg Dwight?

3. What was the name of the 1950s Texan rock 'n' roll singer whose backing band was called the Crickets?

4. For which rock group was Charlie Watts the drummer?

5. What was the name of the best-selling British female group of the 1980s?

6. Which British singer has had a string of hits including 'In the Air Tonight' in 1981, and 'Groovy Kind of Love' in 1988?

7. Who is the connection between the Boomtown Rats and Band Aid?

8. Which rock and soul singer's real name is Annie Mae Bullock?

9. What was the title of Paul Simon's record which topped the album charts in 1986?

10. Which British singer was originally backed by the Shadows?

(See p. 126 for answers)

1   What is the term used to mean treatments such as
    osteopathy and acupuncture?

2   What was first classified into the ABO System in 1902?

3   What does the acronym AIDS stand for?

4   What is the modern name of the disease that was once
    known as 'consumption'?

5   What is the compound added to drinking water to help
    prevent tooth decay?

6   Which parts of the body concern an ENT specialist?

7   Which viral disease attacks the liver in both its 'A' and 'B'
    form?

8   What are affected by presbyopia, astigmatism, myopia and
    cataracts?

9   What is a respiratory disorder caused by allergies,
    infection, stress or emotional upset?

10 What is the condition caused by a shortage of haemoglobin
    in the blood?

(See p. 126 for answers)

Astronomy

1   What is the unit of time based on the orbit of the Earth around the Sun?

2   Which comet will not be visible again from Earth until 2061?

3   Which is the smallest of the nine named planets?

4   What form most of the moon's topographical features?

5   What can be described as 'partial', 'total', 'lunar' and 'solar'?

6   How would an astronomer express 'the distance travelled by a beam of light in a vacuum over 365 days'?

7   Which constellation of the southern hemisphere appears on the national flag of Australia?

8   Which two planets in the Solar System do not have moons?

9   What is thought to be at the centre of a quasar, from which nothing can escape – not even light?

10 What is the popular name for the constellation also known as 'The Big Dipper', 'The Great Bear' and 'Ursa Major'?

(See p. 127 for answers)

True or False?   34

1   The mangelwurzel is a nickname for a scarecrow. True or false?

2   Chopin was a French composer. True or false?

3   Socrates, the great Greek philosopher, never wrote anything down. True or false?

4   The Arctic continent is one of the seven in the world. True or false?

5   All toadstools are mushrooms but not all mushrooms are toadstools. True or false?

6   The swastika was traditionally a symbol of good luck. True or false?

7   The chancellor of the Exchequer is the first lord of the Treasury. True or false?

8   Antarctica contains 70% of the world's fresh water. True or false?

9   Scorpions are eight-legged arachnids, like spiders. True or false?

10 King John signed the Magna Carta. True or false?

(See p. 127 for answers)

MODERATE

★ ★

1   Which is the largest island in the West Indies?

2   Which populous country is over 3¹/₂ million square miles in area, of which two-thirds is either mountains or desert?

3   What is the name of the marshy area of France formed by the Rhône delta and is famous for its white horses?

4   What is to Jordan as Beirut is to Lebanon and Damascus to Syria?

5   Which country straddles Europe and Asia, with both parts linked by the Bosporus Bridge?

6   Which Japanese industrial port was the target of the second atom bomb dropped in World War II?

7   Which Pacific state of the USA was called the Sandwich Islands by Captain Cook?

8   42% of which European country is reclaimed land called polder?

9   What number five to make up New York City, and 32 plus the City to make up Greater London?

10   What flows from the Black Forest to the Black Sea and is the second longest river in Europe?

(See p. 128 for answers)

1   What was the surname shared by two US presidents who took office as the result of assassination?

2   Which two Sioux Indian chiefs defeated General Custer at the Battle of Little Bighorn?

3   Which dam blocks the Colorado River at Boulder, forming Lake Meade and linking Arizona with Nevada?

4   The threat of which judicial procedure forced the resignation of President Richard Nixon in 1974?

5   Which oil magnate left his fortune to found a museum and art gallery in Malibu, California?

6   What was the 13-year period between the passing of the 18th and 21st Amendments, notorious for the rise of gangsters and organized crime, known as?

7   Which office was held in the 19th century by James K. Polk, Rutherford B Hayes and Chester A Arthur?

8   Which political scandal resulted in the conviction of John Poindexter and Oliver North?

9   Who was the only president since World War II to hold office without ever being elected?

10 What is the title of the US government official responsible for foreign affairs?

(See p. 128 for answers)

Sport 37

1. Which national sport originated as a religious ritual performed in Shinto shrines?

2. Which team sport has periods of play called 'chukkas'?

3. Which four events constitute the Grand Slam in tennis?

4. Which US basketball team tours the world playing only exhibition matches?

5. What is the multi-discipline event in women's international athletics in which contestants compete over a two-day period?

6. How many of the drivers who finish a Formula One Grand Prix win points?

7. What is the name of the Berkshire village where Queen Anne established a famous racecourse on the heath?

8. Which Australian city has a cricket ground called the Oval?

9. Which national Scottish game is played on ice, with stones?

10. What is to American football as 'diamond' is to baseball?

(See p. 129 for answers)

1   Which US president was shot five days after the end of the American Civil War?

2   What is the name of the British political regime 1649–60 established by Oliver Cromwell?

3   Which country was ruled by the Romanov dynasty 1613–1917?

4   What was the name of the last battle of the Wars of the Roses, fought in 1485?

5   Who were the Celtic-speaking peoples living in France and Belgium during Roman times?

6   Which wife of Henry VIII had already married twice before she became queen, and married for a fourth time after Henry's death?

7   What was the name of the Austrian-born dictator who succeeded Hindenburg as Germany's head of state?

8   Which country's liberalization programme was halted by the invasion of 600,000 Soviet troops in 1968?

9   In which battle did Harold II, the last Saxon king, lose his life?

10 Which Axis Power changed sides during World War II, declaring war on Germany in October 1943?

(See p. 129 for answers)

1   In which town did Isaac Newton attend the grammar school, and Margaret Thatcher attend the local girls' school?

2   What was the surname of the brothers Julian, who founded the World Wildlife Fund (now the Worldwide Fund for Nature), and Aldous, who wrote *Brave New World*?

3   From which of the nine named planets does the mineral tellurium get its name?

4   Which English physicist and mathematician was born in the same year that Galileo died?

5   What caused the death of John Keats, Frédéric Chopin and Emily Brontë?

6   Which Indian city has a style of riding breeches named after it?

7   Why are the names of the 9th, 10th, 11th and 12th months derived from the Latin for 7, 8, 9 and 10?

8   What was devised by Ludwig Zamenhof in 1887 to make worldwide communication easier?

9   Which British city is the home of the National Museum of Photography, Film and Television?

10   What comes between duke and earl in the ranking of British peers?

(See p. 130 for answers)

1   What is Shakespeare's only play to have an English place name in its title?

2   Which annual British literary prize has been won by Salman Rushdie, Kingsley Amis and Anita Brookner?

3   What is a 3-line, 17-syllable Japanese verse-form?

4   What is the title of Franz Kafka's short story in which the hero turns into an insect?

5   Which French author, the son of one of Napoleon's generals, spent 19 years exiled in Guernsey?

6   Which of Swift's novels is an allegorical tale describing travel to lands of giants, miniature people and intelligent horses?

7   What is the surname shared by the author of *Tom Brown's Schooldays* and the poet laureate appointed in 1984?

8   What was the name of the Onondaga chief about whom Longfellow wrote an epic poem?

9   Which novel was set in a bureaucratic totalitarian state, 35 years ahead of the book's publication date?

10 Which English poet was the spouse of the novelist who created Frankenstein?

(See p. 130 for answers)

1   Which Borodin opera was completed by Rimsky-Korsakov and Glazunov after the composer's death?

2   Which country home and opera house hosts an annual summer festival established by John Christie in 1934?

3   What are the 5-note pentatonic, the 6-note whole-tone, the 7-note diatonic and the 13-note chromatic?

4   For which British king did Handel compose the *Water Music* in 1717?

5   What was used to conduct the orchestra before the baton was introduced in the early 19th century?

6   Which instrument do you associate with John Williams, Julian Bream and Andrés Segovia?

7   What are *Peter Grimes* and *Billy Budd*?

8   Which Irish flautist was a member of the Berlin Philharmonic 1969–75 before pursuing a solo career?

9   What is the title of Beethoven's only opera?

10 Which symphony did Dvorák write during his time as director of the National Conservatory in New York?

(See p. 131 for answers)

1   The stage name of the American film star Issur Danielovitch is: a) Richard Widmark b) Burt Lancaster c) Kirk Douglas

2   Bonnie Prince Charlie, the Young Pretender, was born in: a) Italy b) Ireland c) France

3   Which country has the largest Muslim population in the world? a) Indonesia b) India c) Iran

4   Chatsworth House, seat of the Duke of Devonshire, is in the county of: a) Derbyshire b) Dorset c) Devon

5   The heat at the centre of the Sun is: a) 1,500°C b) 15,000°C c) 15,000,000°C

6   The Dead Sea is below sea level by: a) 1,293 ft b) 2,293 ft c) 3,293 ft

7   In Japan, the Shinkansen is: a) a religious rite b) a type of tea c) a train

8   Up to how many times its own height can a flea jump? a) 30 b) 130 c) 330

9   Hurricane Gilbert, which hit the Caribbean in 1988, had winds gusting over: a) 100 mph b) 150 mph c) 200 mph

10 The official language of the Pyrenean country of Andorra is: a) Catalan b) French c) Spanish

(See p. 131 for answers)

1. What is the name of the membrane enclosing the fluid around the fetus?

2. Which part of the eye contains about 137 million light-sensitive cells in one square inch?

3. What is the fluid that lubricates and cushions the movable joints between the bones?

4. Which is the only vein in the body to carry oxygenated blood?

5. What is the ring of bones at the hip called?

6. Which human body organ weighs about 45 pounds?

7. What are the chemicals produced by the endocrine glands to control body functions?

8. What is the more common name for the tympanic membrane?

9. What is the oxygen-carrying protein found in the red blood cells of the body?

10. What is the colourless liquid, consisting of plasma and white cells, which bathes the body tissues?

(See p. 132 for answers)

1   Which character made his debut in the silent film *Plane Crazy* in 1928?

2   By which names were Virginia McMath and Frederick Austerlitz better known?

3   Which film actress starred in *Taxi Driver* and *Bugsy Malone* when she was only 14?

4   What was the stage name of Arthur Stanley Jefferson, the British comic, who made his name as half of a famous duo?

5   Whose use of 'Method acting' made him one of the cinema's most distinctive stars?

6   Which American directed the controversial 1988 film *The Last Temptation of Christ*?

7   Which Japanese director introduced Japanese cinema to Western audiences with his film *Seven Samurai*?

8   What is the generic name for a cowboy film shot in Europe, of which *A Fistful of Dollars* was the first?

9   Which US film actor began his career using the stage name Duke Morrison?

10 Which author wrote the books on which the films *2001: A Space Odyssey* and *2010: Space Odyssey 2* were based?

(See p. 132 for answers)

1   What are the four fundamental forces of nature?

2   What is the branch of science concerning the study of bodies in motion?

3   What is divided into genera in plant and animal classification?

4   What is the name for a three-dimensional curve generated by a line encircling a cylinder at a constant angle?

5   What is the word which means either the strength of an earthquake or the brightness of a star?

6   What is the more common name for oil of vitriol?

7   Where, in the kitchen, would you find the thermoplastic coating PTFE?

8   What is another name for a rhombus whose internal angles are equal?

9   What is measured by a hygrometer and a hygroscope?

10   What is a device in a machine which allows free movement, especially of a rotating shaft in a housing?

(See p. 133 for answers)

1   What is the emblem of Islam, displayed, for example, on the national flags of Turkey, Pakistan and Tunisia?

2   What is the English name for the Danish port of Helsinger, the setting for Shakespeare's *Hamlet*?

3   What is the Italian word for 'scratched drawings' which we apply to unsolicited, public displays of art?

4   Which Portuguese colony was leased from China and will be handed back in 1999?

5   What is Paddy Ashdown's real first name?

6   Which cloth was first manufactured in the French town of Nimes, from which it got its name?

7   Which UK government-funded body has an official symbol of quality called a 'kite' mark?

8   Which country in the Middle East is the Hashemite Kingdom?

9   What did Tsar Alexander III commission from Fabergé in 1884, as the first of a series of presents for the tsarina?

10 Which is the largest country in area in the British Commonwealth?

(See p. 133 for answers)

1   Which Canadian singer/songwriter recorded the albums *Blue* and *Hejira*?

2   What is the real name of Bono, the lead singer of the Irish rock band U2?

3   Who was *Born to Run* in 1975, and *Born in the USA* in 1984?

4   Which group of brothers had their first US hit with 'I Want You Back' in 1969?

5   Which guitarist formed the rock group whose album, *Brothers in Arms*, has sold over 20 million copies?

6   Who collaborated with Andrew Lloyd Webber to write *Joseph and the Amazing Technicolor Dreamcoat*?

7   What was the name of the hard-rock group formed by David Bowie in the late 1980s?

8   Which type of music developed from the folk music of English, Irish and Scottish settlers in the USA?

9   Who wrote the song 'White Christmas' in 1942?

10   Which English rock group had a stage show that often ended with them destroying their instruments?

(See p. 134 for answers)

1   Which sea is so highly polluted that the Barcelona Convention was set up in 1976 to try and clean it up?

2   What are the three main greenhouse gases?

3   What natural feature covers approximately 6% of the Earth's land surface, and harbours 40% of the Earth's species?

4   What was on patrol in the Pacific, protesting against nuclear testing, when it was sunk by French agents in 1985?

5   25% of which traditional British feature was cut down between 1945 and 1985 because of agricultural mechanization?

6   What was the viral disease controversially introduced into Britain during the 1950s to reduce the rabbit population?

7   Who was director of the environmental pressure group Friends of the Earth 1984–90?

8   Which European country is committed to decommissioning all of its nuclear reactors?

9   Which inland sea between Kazakhstan and Uzbekistan is fast disappearing because the rivers that feed it have been diverted and dammed?

10 What is the name of Britain's nuclear-fuel reprocessing plant?

(See p. 134 for answers)

1 The Roman emperor Hadrian was born in Italy. True or false?

2 In the Netherlands, all governments since 1945 have been coalitions. True or false?

3 The French eat an average of 11 pounds of snails per head per year. True or false?

4 The hands and feet contain almost half the bones in the human body. True or false?

5 There are three goals at each end in Australian Rules football. True or false?

6 A mudskipper fish often climbs out of the water, and skips away when alarmed. True or false?

7 British MPs have always received a salary. True or false?

8 P G Wodehouse collaborated with Kern and Gershwin to write Broadway musicals. True or false?

9 Giant worms over 6 ft long live at the bottom of the sea beside hydrothermal vents called smokers. True or false?

10 Washington, Jefferson, Lincoln and Grant are the four Presidents' heads sculpted into Mount Rushmore. True or false?

(See p. 135 for answers)

UK Politics 50

1   Which Conservative MP was a middle-distance runner who won two Olympic gold medals and set 11 world records during the 1970s and 1980s?

2   In which year was the voting age reduced from 21 to 18?

3   Which prime minister took Britain into the European Community in 1973?

4   What became known as 'the F-word' at the 1991 Maastricht Summit, where Britain wanted it removed from the Treaty?

5   Which document was drawn up and unveiled by John Major in 1991 in an effort to raise standards for consumers and improve public services?

6   Who succeeded Clement Attlee as Labour Party leader in 1955?

7   What is the title of the presiding officer who keeps order in the House of Commons?

8   Which British actress won the Hampstead and Highgate seat for Labour in the 1992 General Election?

9   What is the term used when a sitting MP is removed as the candidate for a forthcoming election?

10 What is the Swedish word for 'commissioner' which refers to the official who investigates citizens' complaints against the government?

(See p. 135 for answers)

1   Which plant of the carrot family has stems that are crystallized and used in baking and cake decoration?

2   What is the salt solution used for curing meat and canning vegetables?

3   Which controversial process was introduced in the 1980s to prolong the life of foodstuffs?

4   What is the German word for 'store' and is the name we give to a light beer?

5   What does the abbreviation UHT stand for?

6   Which strong cheese, made from ewe's milk and stored in caves, is named after a village in France?

7   Which grain is said to be the staple food of more than one-third of the world's population?

8   What are the black fruits that produce monounsaturated oil when pressed?

9   What is the process that rids food, especially milk, of bacteria?

10 Which berries are used to give gin its flavour?

(See p. 136 for answers)

1   Which family of insects has species named 'drivers', 'weavers' and even individuals called 'soldiers'?

2   Which digestive organ is well-developed in grass-eating herbivores, but is only vestigial in humans?

3   What are the nocturnal, herding herbivores of Australia, Tasmania and New Guinea?

4   Which insects' larvae secrete blobs of froth called 'cuckoo spit'?

5   Which are the only birds able to fly backwards?

6   Which rodent rears its young, called kittens, in a nest called a drey?

7   What is the most abundant substance in the plant kingdom, which no mammal produces the enzyme to digest?

8   Which protected animal eats a diet of about 2lb of eucalyptus shoots every day?

9   What grow as parasites and saprotrophs, contain no chlorophyll, and reproduce by means of spores?

10   What type of seaweed grows up to 320 ft in length, and is farmed for its alginates?

(See p. 136 for answers)

1   In which town were the investitures of Edward VIII and Prince Charles held, when each was created Prince of Wales?

2   What was the first name shared by Lord Kitchener and Lord Nelson?

3   Which is the only French-speaking Republic in the Americas?

4   Who is buried at the Hôtel des Invalides in Paris?

5   In which year was the British Commonwealth established?

6   What is the Russian word for 'dissolute' and the nick-name given to Grigory Efimovich, the illiterate son of a peasant, who had influence over the tsarina?

7   In which city was the world's first skyscraper built?

8   In which building was Winston Churchill born in 1874?

9   What is a unit of thermal insulation used in the textile trade and is often associated with duvets?

10 Which body of people is sometimes referred to as 'The Fourth Estate'?

(See p. 137 for answers)

Art and Architecture 54

1 Which Swiss painter taught at the Bauhaus school during the 1920s?

2 Who was the architect of The Guggenheim Museum in New York?

3 What took Michelangelo four years to complete because, most of the time, he was having to work leaning backwards?

4 What style of English architecture is described as 'Early English', 'Decorated' and 'Perpendicular'?

5 How do we refer to the group of late 19th-century artists who depicted real life, nature and light in their paintings?

6 Which artist became famous through his posters of Parisian entertainers and prostitutes?

7 Which English artist began his career as a medical illustrator, but is best known for his paintings of horses?

8 What was the extravagant style of art and architecture that dominated Europe during most of the 17th century?

9 What is the title of the painting by Picasso inspired by the bombing of civilians in the Spanish Civil War?

10 Which American artist was a pioneer of Abstract Expressionism, and a leading exponent of action painting?

(See p. 137 for answers)

1   Which toxic, crystalline metalloid has the chemical symbol As?

2   What is alloyed with copper to make bronze, and with lead to make pewter?

3   What is the scale of hardness on which talc registers one and diamond ten?

4   Which substance, used in medicine, photography and making dyes, gives off a violet vapour when heated?

5   What aptly describes all transuranic elements?

6   What is the common name for solid carbon dioxide?

7   What is the process in which a solid changes to a vapour without passing through the liquid stage?

8   Which metal is produced from the ores limonite, hematite and magnetite?

9   What is the collective name for the five elements which make up Group VII of the periodic table?

10 What is the name for the green-blue coating that forms naturally on copper, bronze and brass?

(See p. 138 for answers)

1   Which American pioneer of modern dance died when her long scarf caught in the wheel of a car?

2   What was the name of the American showman who established 'The Greatest Show on Earth' in 1871?

3   With what do you associate Frederick Ashton, Ninette de Valois and Marie Rambert?

4   Which Swiss lakeside resort has an annual television festival whose top award is The Golden Rose?

5   Who appeared in the Oxford revue *Beyond The Fringe* and went on to open a satirical nightclub called The Establishment?

6   What was the screen name of Lee Yuen Kam?

7   Who wrote the lyrics for Leonard Bernstein's musical *West Side Story*?

8   Which London theatre began life as the Coburg, but should really be known as the Royal Victoria Hall?

9   Which playwright wrote the controversial television play *Brimstone and Treacle* in 1976, but found it banned from transmission until 1987?

10   Who is the film star brother of the actress who starred in *Terms of Endearment* and *Steel Magnolias*?

(See p. 138 for answers)

1   When did Canberra become the Australian capital? a) 1878
    b) 1908 c) 1928

2   The Japanese word meaning 'empty hand' is: a) kungfu
    b) karate c) kendo

3   The approximate distance in miles between the Earth and
    the Sun is: a) 9,000,000 b) 90,000,000 c) 900,000,000

4   The last king of Albania was called: a) King Xog b) King
    Yog c) King Zog

5   The human body contains: a) 106 bones b) 156 bones
    c) 206 bones

6   Moscow's underground system, the Metro, carries
    approximately how many passengers per day?
    a) 1,500,000 b) 6,500,000 c) 16,500,000

7   According to the Old Testament, how old was Methuselah
    when he died? a) 696 yrs b) 969 yrs c) 996 yrs

8   Which sport had its first set of rules drawn up in 1848; its
    Association founded in 1863; and its League formed in
    1888? a) rugby b) cricket c) football

9   Mount Ararat is in present-day: a) Turkey b) Israel c) Syria

10 In helping Bonnie Prince Charlie escape to France, Flora
    Macdonald disguised him as: a) her sister b) her tutor
    c) her maid

See p. 139 for answers)

1   What is the name for the area of north Staffordshire where the Wedgwood and Minton factories are situated?

2   Which island and ferry port is connected to Anglesey by road and rail bridges?

3   Which is the largest lake in the British Isles?

4   Through which Yorkshire city does the river Don flow?

5   Which is the only English island county?

6   Which range of hills forms a natural border between England and Scotland?

7   Which city is the second largest in the UK?

8   What was the name of the Roman road that ran from London to Chester?

9   What is the name given to longitude 0°, from which the world's standard time zones are calculated?

10 In which range of mountains is Aviemore, the Scottish winter sports centre, situated?

(See p. 139 for answers)

1   Who were the guardian spirits of nature in Greek mythology?

2   What was left as a consolation inside Pandora's box?

3   What was the name of the 'river of hate' that flowed round the Underworld?

4   Which animals are thought to have given rise to the belief in mermaids?

5   Who was endowed with the gift of prophecy by Apollo, but fated never to be believed?

6   Which Cornish village is said to be the birthplace of King Arthur?

7   Who was the siren who sat on a rock in the Rhine and lured sailors to their deaths?

8   What was the food of the gods, said to give eternal life to those who ate it?

9   What was the condition which Orpheus failed to fulfil in bringing Eurydice back to life from Hades, because the temptation was too great?

10 Which handsome god was killed by a twig of mistletoe in Norse mythology?

(See p. 140 for answers)

Physics

1   What is an unchanging position in which forces cancel each other out?

2   What does c represent in the equation $e = mc^2$?

3   What can be expressed as the number of cycles of a vibration occurring per unit of time?

4   What is measured by the SI unit called a 'henry'?

5   What does the abbreviation STP stand for?

6   What is commonly used in a rectifier to convert alternating current to direct current?

7   What is the product of the mass of a body and its linear velocity?

8   What is the force that opposes the relative motion of two bodies that are in contact?

9   What is a cylindrical coil of wire in which a magnetic field is created when an electric current is passed through it?

10 What is the study and use of frequencies above 20 khz?

(See p. 140 for answers)

1　Which structures have four basic designs – beam, cantilever, arch and suspension?

2　What is the popular name for members of the RCMP?

3　Which sign is the decapod of the zodiac?

4　What is the collective word for a group of companies that limits competition by price-fixing, market-sharing and restricting output?

5　In which Soviet Republic was the space-launch site, the Baikonur Cosmodrome, built?

6　Which country has problems with the drug barons of Medellín?

7　Which Wiltshire country house, famous for its Safari Park lions, is the seat of Lord Bath?

8　What are the substances in the saliva of vampire bats, leeches and mosquitoes which stop blood from clotting?

9　Which type of edible nut is produced by a variety of hickory tree?

10　What was the name of the pope who introduced the reformed calendar used by the Western world?

(See p. 141 for answers)

1   What comprise the Decalogue?

2   Which two priceless resins were brought by the Magi to the infant Jesus?

3   What were the names of Noah's three sons?

4   Which of the New Testament gospels is not synoptic?

5   Who was the son of Jesse, father of Solomon and second King of Israel?

6   Who is the false god, representing greed and wealth, cited in the New Testament?

7   Which disciple was a tax collector before being called to follow Jesus?

8   Which five books of the Old Testament make up the Pentateuch?

9   What is the collective word for the writers of the four Gospels?

10   Who was first to meet the risen Jesus after the Crucifixion?

(See p. 141 for answers)

1   Which planet takes almost 30 Earth years to orbit the Sun?

2   What travels around the Sun at an average speed of 185 miles per second?

3   Which astronomer established that the Sun, not the Earth, was the centre of the solar system?

4   What is almost halfway through its 10-billion-year life, will expand to become a red giant and then shrink to become a white dwarf?

5   What was the name of two space probes launched in 1977 which sent back remarkable pictures of Jupiter, Saturn, Uranus and Neptune?

6   Which planet orbits the Sun four times in the time it takes the Earth to go round once?

7   What are the clouds of interstellar dust, said to be the birthplace of stars?

8   What is the Latin name for the North Star?

9   What is the astronomical unit equal to 32.616 light years?

10   What are the two contradicting theories explaining how the universe was created and evolved?

(See p. 142 for answers)

1   What colour is a 'black box' flight recorder?

2   What was the name of the ship in which Captain Scott and his expedition sailed to the Antarctic in 1900?

3   What form of transport was initially a form of hobby-horse?

4   What was the name of the three-stage rocket used in the Apollo series of moonshots?

5   Which two British engineers got together in 1905 to design and produce cars?

6   What term denotes the communications and weather satellites that appear to stay above one point on the Earth?

7   Which American aviator was the first woman to fly the Atlantic solo in 1932?

8   Which type of Ford car was the first to be constructed by mass production, in 1908?

9   What is the name of the industrial city on Honshu Island, Japan, and also that of a motorcycle manufactured there?

10   What do Americans call the jet fuel paraffin?

(See p. 142 for answers)

1 Who pioneered the use of antiseptics, which resulted in a dramatic reduction in the death rate during surgery?

2 What is the term for a physical change resulting from disease or injury?

3 What is the viral disease, named after a West African village, for which there is no known cure?

4 What is the Latin for 'I will please', a word used to mean a sugar pill that has no active effect?

5 What is the common name for the infectious disease whose medical name is rubeola?

6 What is the antimalarial drug extracted from the bark of the cinchona tree?

7 Which species of macaque monkey gave its name to the blood-group system of humans?

8 Which viral disease, once endemic in Europe, was eradicated worldwide in 1980?

9 What is the pneumonia-like disease named after the people who caught it while attending an American Convention in Philadelphia in 1976?

10 What has the technical name dyspepsia, a disorder causing abdominal pain?

(See p. 143 for answers)

1   What was the name of the prophet on whose book Joseph Smith founded the Church of Latter-day Saints?

- 2   The name of which religion translates as 'submission'?

3   Where did St Bernadette experience a vision of the Virgin Mary in 1858?

4   Which colourful festival is celebrated on and named after Shrove Tuesday, the day before the Lenten fast?

5   Who is the spiritual leader of the Tibetan Buddhists?

6   Which movement within the Christian Church is working towards its eventual reunification?

7   What is the informal name for the members of the Unification Church, founded by a Korean in 1954?

8   Who calls the Muslim faithful to prayer, five times a day, from the minaret of a mosque?

9   Which Christian religious order was founded by Ignatius Loyola?

10   What is the indigenous religion of Japan?

(See p. 143 for answers)

1 In 1989 the remains of which 17th-century theatre were discovered and excavated near Southwark Bridge?

2 What is the Italian word for 'swank' and the name of an organization that is also known as La Cosa Nostra?

3 Who used the Latin phrase 'cogito ergo sum' ('I think therefore I am') as the foundation for his philosophical theory?

4 Which language is related to both Cornish and Welsh, and is now a recognized language of France?

5 What is the name for all citizens born and brought up in the Western Isles?

6 Which river is poetically called 'Isis' until it flows through Oxford?

7 In which European city are the headquarters of the Red Cross?

8 Which two sets of exams were replaced by the GCSE in 1988?

9 Who was commissioned to redesign 51 London churches burned down in the Great Fire of 1666?

10 What is an important meeting between world political leaders usually called?

(See p. 144 for answers)

HARD

★ ★ ★

1   What is the name of the trench in the Pacific Ocean which is the lowest place on the Earth's surface?

2   In which African country is the town of Timbuktu?

3   Which group of South Atlantic Islands was named after a 17th-century treasurer of the British navy?

4   Which historic city is Italy's main port?

5   What is the collective name for the eastern region of the Mediterranean, consisting of the coastal regions of Syria, Lebanon, Israel and Turkey?

6   In which American state are the sources of the Red River, St Lawrence River and the Mississippi River?

7   Which Russian seaport is the largest city within the Arctic Circle, with a population of 432,000?

8   In which country is the highest waterfall in the world, the Angel Falls, at 3,210 ft?

9   What is the name for the rocky debris eroded, carried along and deposited by glaciers?

10   Which country's capital is situated on a tributary of the Murrumbidgcc River?

(See p. 144 for answers)

1   Which Dutch graphic artist painted pictures of visual paradoxes and optical illusions?

2   Which German architect founded the Bauhaus School in 1919?

3   What is the collective name for the three goddesses who are said to be the personifications of pleasure, charm and beauty?

4   Who designed the Cenotaph in Whitehall?

5   Which 17th-century artist painted more than 60 self-portraits?

6   Which family's art treasures became the basis of the collection at the Uffizi Gallery in Florence?

7   Who became the first president of the Royal Academy in 1768?

8   What was designed by the architect Sir Joseph Paxton to house the Great Exhibition of 1851?

9   Which French artist was best known for his streetscapes of Paris?

10   Which British artist painted a series of screaming popes based on a portrait of Innocent X by Velázquez?

(See p. 145 for answers)

1 Memphis was the name of an early capital of Egypt. True or false?

2 The laws of the United Kingdom are based on a written constitution kept at the Houses of Parliament. True or false?

3 William the Conqueror was the illegitimate son of Robert the Devil, Duke of Normandy. True or false?

4 Isaac Newton, the mathematician and physicist, was a Whig MP. True or false?

5 The South Orkneys is the name of a group of islands off the north coast of Scotland. True or false?

6 The numbat is a marsupial and rears its young in a pouch. True or false?

7 Stephenson's locomotive *Rocket* pulled the first public steam train from Stockton to Darlington in 1825. True or false?

8 An 'inferno' is a unit of heat equal to 1 billion K (about 1 billion°C). True or false?

9 Squirrels, beavers, chipmunks and porcupines are all rodents. True or false?

10 The group of long-established US universities known as the Ivy League is so named because each one had the emblem of an ivy leaf. True or false?

(See p. 145 for answers)

1 Where did Florence Nightingale establish a hospital to treat casualties of the Crimean War?

2 What was the name of the Libyan king deposed by Colonel Khaddhafi in 1969?

3 Who was the admiral of the French fleet defeated by Nelson at the Battle of Trafalgar?

4 What was ceded to Britain in 1713 as part of the settlement of the War of Spanish Succession?

5 Who was the queen of the British king Charles I?

6 What was the name of the basalt slab that became the key for deciphering ancient Egyptian hieroglyphics?

7 Which US president ended his country's participation in the Vietnam War?

8 Which two Britons met at Ujiji, Tanganyika, on 10 November 1871?

9 What Soviet 'man of steel' was educated for the priesthood but was expelled from the seminary?

10 Who succeeded Henry I as king of England in 1135?

(See p. 146 for answers)

1 What is the title of the play that chronicles a day in the life of the small Welsh village of Llareggub?

2 Whose name is synonymous with *Le Grand Dictionnaire Universel du XIXème Siècle*?

3 Which of King Lear's three daughters was murdered?

4 Which poet laureate wrote the biography *The Life of Nelson* in 1813?

5 What is the term applied to the unrhymed, iambic pentameter used by Shakespeare in all his plays?

6 Which English poet was the Latin secretary to Oliver Cromwell's Council of State during the Commonwealth period?

7 Which 16th-century English dramatist was imprisoned for murder, and was himself murdered in a tavern brawl?

8 Who wrote an elegy on Abraham Lincoln called 'When Lilacs Last in the Dooryard Bloom'd'?

9 Which phrase refers to the group of British writers that included Colin Wilson, Kingsley Amis, John Braine and Alan Sillitoe?

10 Which British prime minister wrote the novel trilogy *Coningsby*, *Sybil* and *Tancred*?

(See p. 146 for answers)

Biology

1 What has a central vein called a midrib?

2 The male of which Arctic whale has a single, spirally-fluted tusk that can be up to 9 ft long?

3 What is the name of the lustrous substance that forms pearl and mother-of-pearl?

4 Which acid is contained in rhubarb leaves, making them poisonous to eat?

5 What do amoebas do by binary fission?

6 What is the Latin word for 'liquid' which we use to mean the fluid produced by the tree *Ficus elastica*?

7 Which antipodean bird is the largest member of the kingfisher family?

8 What is the generic word for plants that grow in water or water-logged conditions?

9 What is the state of inactivity through the dry, summer season, as hibernation is the dormancy of the winter months?

10 Which mammal constructs a lodge in which to store food, rear young and pass the winter?

(See p. 147 for answers)

1   What is known in the USA as 'off-off Broadway'?

2   What was the nickname of the Marx brother who left the zany group before any films were made?

3   In which type of Japanese drama do men take all the parts ... in the interests of propriety?

4   Who co-founded the Renaissance Theatre Company with David Parfitt in 1987?

5   Which two brothers collaborated to write the opera *Porgy and Bess*?

6   Whose book *The Wonderful Wizard of Oz* was made into the film starring Judy Garland?

7   Which entertainer began his career as dancing partner to Mistinguett at the Folies Bergère?

8   Which Scottish music-hall singer started out as an 'Irish' comedian?

9   Who was the jazz clarinettist nicknamed 'The King of Swing'?

10 Which two people were *Waiting for Godot*, in the play by Samuel Beckett?

(See p. 147 for answers)

1 What is the general term for the use of computers, telecommunications and microelectronics in the processing and transmission of data?

2 What is the name of the South African movement led by Chief Buthelezi?

3 Which was the first day of the year in the Roman calendar?

4 To which royal house does the royal family of Monaco belong?

5 Which London church is officially the Collegiate Church of St Peter?

6 Who is excluded from succession to the throne in Salic Law?

7 Which boy's name, signalled in Morse code, would be represented by six dashes?

8 What is the study of the relationship between people and their working environment, with the aim of improving performance?

9 Which diamond has a Persian name meaning 'mountain of light'?

10 What do the Sikhs propose to call their separate state, if it ever achieves independence from India?

(See p. 148 for answers)

1 Which milk pudding is made from starch extracted from the pith of a palm tree?

2 Which vegetable is a green variety of banana, used as a staple food in the tropics?

3 Which cereal is used to make 'black' breads?

4 Which cheese is traditionally made around Melton Mowbray, and gets its name from the village where the cheeses were taken for transporting to London?

5 What accurately describes drinks with no C_2H_5OH content?

6 What is the secondary covering of a nutmeg?

7 For what are thaumatin, aspartame and manitol used as substitutes?

8 What sort of high-gluten flour is used for making pasta?

9 What type of flowers produce vanilla pods?

10 What are the dried stigmas of crocus flowers, used as a flavouring and colouring?

(See p. 148 for answers)

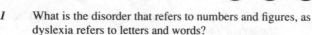

1   What is the disorder that refers to numbers and figures, as dyslexia refers to letters and words?

2   What is the condition, more common in men than women, caused by an accumulation of uric acid crystals in the joints?

3   What is the chronic, progressive, tropical disease, sometimes called Hansen's Disease?

4   What is caused by the blockage of a blood vessel by a blood clot, fat particle or bubble of air?

5   What is the chemical, produced naturally in the brain cells, the lack of which causes Parkinson's Disease?

6   What gas, forming bubbles in the blood of a diver returning too quickly to the surface, causes the decompression sickness known as 'the bends'?

7   What is the extract of peppermint used as an antiseptic, inhalant and analgesic?

8   Which system of the body is affected by Hodgkins' Disease?

9   What can be made from nylon, gut or wire, and is used for 'tying off' in surgery?

10   Which US physician developed a vaccine that virtually eradicated polio in the industrialized countries?

(See p. 149 for answers)

1   Which composer held the office of prime minister in Poland in 1919?

2   What was the name of the Italian village renowned for its violin-making familes of Amati, Guarneri and Stradivari?

3   Which composer transcribed birdsong and incorporated it into much of his work?

4   Whose operas are performed at the annual summer festival at Bayreuth in Germany?

5   Which legendary magician was the inspiration for musical works by Busoni, Berlioz, Gounod and Schumann?

6   To which family of instruments does the double bass belong?

7   Which Australian composer, pianist and organist has held the post of Master of the Queen's Music since 1975?

8   What was the surname of the Austrian who catalogued Mozart's works with K-numbers?

9   Which composer was Kapellmeister to Prince Esterhazy 1761–90?

10   Which British conductor founded 'the Proms' in 1895?

(See p. 149 for answers)

1 What creatures do wild bananas depend on for pollination?
a) bats b) humming birds c) butterflies

2 Maurice Micklewhite is the real name of the film actor:
a) Terence Stamp b) Bob Hoskins c) Michael Caine

3 The first British Open Golf Championship was held in:
a) 1860 b) 1880 c) 1900

4 The loganberry was named after: a) Mount Logan in
Canada where it was found b) The US judge James H
Logan who grew it c) Logan Farm in Scotland, where it
was cultivated

5 Karaoke is the Japanese word meaning: a) plain singing
b) empty orchestra c) backing music

6 What bird family does the peacock belong to? a) pheasant
b) kingfisher c) bird of paradise

7 How many wives did Henry VIII have beheaded? a) two
b) four c) six

8 The worldwide total of nuclear weapons in 1990 was:
a) 5,000 b) 15,000 c) 50,000

9 The world's largest producer of wine is: a) Italy
b) Bulgaria c) France

10 How many bicycles are said to be used in the world today?
a) 800 million b) 8 billion c) 8 trillion

(See p. 150 for answers)

1   What discovery, made by Alec Jeffreys in the mid-1980s, is now used as a means of identification?

2   What is the study of electronic systems that can perform the functions of living beings?

3   Which Russian chemist devised the first form of the periodic table in 1869?

4   Which English naturalist, concurrently and independently, arrived at a theory of evolution similar to that of Darwin?

5   What natural organism is used to obtain litmus dye, used as an indicator in chemistry?

6   What describes a triangle whose three sides are all of different lengths?

7   What is the prefix denoting 'multiplied by 10 to the power 6'?

8   What is said to have been invented by Charles Babbage when he designed his 'analytical engine' in 1833?

9   What is the major ore of uranium?

10 Which French chemist gave oxygen its name and proved that water was a compound of oxygen and hydrogen?

(See p. 150 for answers)

1 Which two sports use mallets?

2 Which English League soccer club had Ian Botham on its books from 1979 to 1984?

3 What is the name of the most famous Highland Games held in a village near Balmoral Castle?

4 In American football, what do AFC and NFC stand for?

5 Name one of the two types of canoe used in competitive canoeing.

6 Which two sports are played on oval pitches?

7 How many innings are allowed for each team in baseball?

8 In which sport is the Webb Ellis Cup presented to the winners of the World Cup?

9 In which four events did Jesse Owens, in 1936, and Carl Lewis, in 1984, win gold medals?

10 What has no brakes, no steering mechanism, and is used in a sport contested in the winter Olympics?

(See p. 151 for answers)

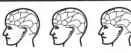

1. What is the ancient Greek name for Troy, from which the title of an epic Homeric poem is derived?

2. What is the Spanish title equivalent to that of a British princess?

3. In which river valley was gold discovered in the Yukon in 1896, causing 30,000 prospectors to rush to the area?

4. What is the name for a Japanese gangster in organized crime, a word meaning 'good for nothing'?

5. Which sign of the zodiac was once part of the adjacent sign, Scorpio?

6. What is identified by its ISBN?

7. On which everyday object would you find the inscriptions 'Decus et tutamen'; 'Nemo me impune lacessit'; or 'Pleidiol wyf i'm gwlad'?

8. What is the collective term for the Spanish, Romanian, Portuguese, Italian and French languages?

9. How do you notate 'multiply by one thousand' in Roman numerals?

10. Who was the author of the Mary Poppins stories?

(See p. 151 for answers)

1   Which of the gospel writers also wrote the Acts of the Apostles?

2   What was the language spoken 2,000 years ago in Palestine, and used by Jesus?

3   Who was John the Baptist's mother?

4   Which section of the Bible was written in Greek during the 1st and 2nd centuries?

5   To which race of non-Semitic people did Delilah belong?

6   The reigns of which two kings are chronicled in the two books of Samuel?

7   What was the name of Naomi's daughter-in-law?

8   Which prophetess of the Old Testament led an army of Israelites to victory over the Canaanites?

9   What was the clerical office held by John when he wrote his three New Testament Epistles?

10   Which two books of the Old Testament have female names as titles?

(See p. 152 for answers)

1. What is the name of the Alaskan channel in which the *Exxon Valdez* caused one of the world's greatest shipping oil spillage disasters in 1989?

2. What is formed in bogs by the incomplete decomposition of sphagnum moss, and only grows 1 mm a year?

3. Which country would suffer devastating effects as a result of global warming, because 75% of its 55,000 square miles is less than 10 ft above sea level?

4. Which European country uses its subterranean thermal water to heat 85% of its homes?

5. Which landlocked Asian country is described as 'the world's highest rubbish dump' because of all the refuse left behind by expeditions?

6. What is caused by the release of sulphur dioxide into the atmosphere?

7. On which group of British islands is Burgar Hill, where the world's most productive wind-powered generator is situated?

8. Which highly polluted Italian river discharges 234 tonnes of arsenic into the sea a year?

9. Which capital city has less green space than any other European capital and severe air pollution that is destroying the Classical buildings?

10. Which was the first national park, established in the USA in 1872?
(See p. 152 for answers)

1   Which state is known as 'The Land of Enchantment'?

2   What was the name of the commission set up to investigate the assassination of President Kennedy?

3   Which one of the five Great Lakes lies totally within the United States?

4   Who was President of the Screen Actors' Guild in America 1947–52?

5   What are collectively known as the Bill of Rights?

6   In which city is the University of California situated?

7   Which astronaut remained in the orbiting command module while Neil Armstrong first set foot on the moon?

8   What was transported from England in 1971 and has now become a big tourist attraction in Lake Havasu City, Arizona?

9   What was the codename for the development of the atom bomb in World War II?

10   Which President was actually impeached, but the Senate failed to convict him … by one vote?

(See p. 153 for answers)

True or False?

1 The basic unit of currency in Egypt, Lebanon and Syria is the dinar. True or false?

2 The Russian parliament building in Moscow is called the White House. True or false?

3 The engine which powered the Sinclair C5 was a washing-machine motor. True or false?

4 Chinook, Sirocco, Harmattan and Mistral are all names of helicopters. True or false?

5 Tartans were banned after the Jacobite rebellion of 1745 until 1782. True or false?

6 The jackal-headed god Anubis guided the souls of the dead in ancient Egypt. True or false?

7 Roman soldiers were paid part of their salary in salt. True or false?

8 Only female wasps sting. True or false?

9 Kenneth MacAlpin united the kingdoms of Scotland in the 9th century. True or false?

10 Tokyo has a Disney theme park. True or false?

(See p. 153 for answers)

1   Which oxide expands by one-eleventh of its volume when frozen?

2   What is a very hard, naturally-occurring mineral, of which ruby and sapphire are gem-quality varieties?

3   Which element has the highest melting point of any metal at 3,410°C?

4   What are formed by the condensation reaction of dibasic acids and polyhydric alcohols?

5   Which is the densest known gas?

6   Which metal of the platinum group is twice as heavy as lead?

7   What is the chief ore of mercury?

8   What does the abbreviation PVC stand for?

9   What is the technique of analytical chemistry for finding the concentration of a dissolved compound by using a reagent?

10   What has a molecule of six carbon atoms formed into the shape of a ring, with six hydrogen atoms attached?

(See p. 154 for answers)

1. What is the title of the member of the upper house equivalent to that of the Speaker in the lower house?

2. What is the collective name of the international agreements signed by all the member states of the European Community?

3. Which MP entered Parliament as a Tory in 1833, but became Liberal prime minister in 1868?

4. Who preceded Norman Lamont as chancellor of the Exchequer?

5. What is the other post held by the minister who is also chancellor of the Duchy of Lancaster in a Conservative cabinet?

6. Who was the first party leader in British politics to be elected by party members who were not MPs?

7. What was enforced by parliament in 1379 and was the trigger that caused the Peasants' Revolt?

8. In what year did the Representation of the People Act give the vote to all women over 21?

9. Which county has a Tinners' Parliament called the Stannary, whose rights have never been rescinded by Westminster?

10. The secretary of state for which government ministry has responsibility for the council tax?

(See p. 154 for answers)

1   What was the name taken by Nicholas Breakspear in 1154 when he became the only English pope?

2   According to the Jewish Talmud, who was Adam's first wife, before God created Eve?

3   What is the title of either of the two epic Hindu poems written in Sanskrit?

4   Which religion has observances known as the 'Five Pillars of Faith', binding to all adult male believers?

5   What is the name of the process, culminating in a ceremony at St Peter's basilica in Rome, by which a member of the Catholic church achieves full sainthood?

6   Which archbishop holds the official title 'Primate of England'?

7   What is the meaning of the name 'Christ'?

8   What religion, founded in the 19th century, holds that all great religious leaders are manifestations of an unknowable God, that all scriptures are sacred, and that its members must teach this and work for world unification?

9   Which is the ninth month of the Muslim calendar?

10 Which philosophical religion believes that the universe is kept in balance by the opposing forces of yin and yang?

(See p. 155 for answers)

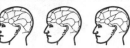

1. Of which country is the wattle the national emblem?
2. What was traditionally followed by a beating of the skin with birch twigs, and a roll in the snow?
3. What is the name of the Oxford college founded in 1899 to provide education for working people?
4. What is the name of the world tree that spans heaven and hell in Norse mythology?
5. Which two people, a British fashion designer and a rock music entrepreneur, started the punk movement of the 1970s?
6. What was Jacqueline Kennedy's maiden name?
7. What is the acronym for an independent organization, such as the Equal Opportunities Commission, set up by the government and relying on it for funds?
8. What is the Russian word for 'peace' and the name of the Soviet space station launched in 1986?
9. Where was Nelson Mandela held in prison for 27 years?
10. Which British crown dependency has a government called the Court of Tynwald?

(See p. 155 for answers)

1   Which of the first six planets in our solar system is the only one to spin in an east-to-west direction?

2   What did the American Edwin Hubble classify as 'spirals', 'barred spirals' and 'ellipticals'?

3   Which planet has one moon called Charon?

4   What is the name given to the two zones of charged particles around the Earth's magnetosphere?

5   What is the change in the apparent position of an astronomical object against its background, when viewed from two different points?

6   Which constellation contains the supergiant star Betelgeuse?

7   What is the largest asteroid, orbiting the Sun every 46 years?

8   On which planet is the Earth-sized, oval storm cloud called the Great Dark Spot?

9   Which galaxy is 2.2 million light years away, and the most distant object visible to the naked eye?

10 Which of the nine planets contains twice as much mass as all the other planets combined?

(See p. 156 for answers)

1 Which film star did the Canadian Gladys Mary Smith grow up to be?

2 Who directed *The Godfather* in 1972 and its two sequels in 1974 and 1990?

3 What was the title of the film in which Charlie Chaplin spoke for the first time?

4 Which newspaper magnate was the model for Orson Welles's *Citizen Kane*?

5 What were the animals in the title of the film which won an Oscar for Best Picture in the 1990 Academy Awards?

6 Who was *Desperately Seeking Susan* in her first film in 1985?

7 Which film director is said to have invented montage in his films *Alexander Nevsky* and *Battleship Potemkin*?

8 Which actor did Mae West choose as her co-star for the film *She Done Him Wrong*?

9 What was the title of the big box-office flop that almost caused the collapse of United Artists in 1980?

10 Who played Bonnie Parker opposite Warren Beatty's Clyde Barrow in the 1967 film *Bonnie and Clyde*?

(See p. 156 for answers)

1   Which organ helps to process white blood cells, destroys old red blood cells, and stores iron?

2   What are the natural pain-killing substances produced in the brain and pituitary gland?

3   What is an overgrowth of fibrous tissue, usually produced at the site of a scar?

4   Which protein forms hair and nails?

5   What is the coloured muscle that responds involuntarily to light?

6   What is the substance produced by hard exercise and oxygen debt, causing stiffness in the muscles?

7   Which three bones are collectively known as the auditory ossicles?

8   What is the pigment that colours skin?

9   Of what do we have 52 in a lifetime, 20 of which are deciduous?

10 What is the substance that the body over-produces in an allergic reaction to pollen?

(See p. 157 for answers)

1   Who, in Hindu mythology, is the wife of Siva and the
     goddess of death and destruction?

2   From which sun goddess did all Japanese emperors claim
     to be descended?

3   What was the name of Zeus's shield?

4   Where were unicorns said to live?

5   Who fell in love with a statue he had carved?

6   What is the collective name for the three goddesses
     Clotho, Lachesis and Atropos who controlled human
     destiny according to the ancient Greeks?

7   In Norse mythology, where is the home of the gods,
     reached by crossing the rainbow bridge?

8   Which nymphs in Greek mythology were the guardian
     spirits of the sea?

9   Who is the Chinese and Japanese mother goddess, whose
     attributes are compassion and mercy, and who is a form of
     the bodhisattva Avalokiteśvara?

10   What was the name for the 'Islands of the Blessed' where
     heroes were sent by the Greek gods to enjoy a life after
     death?

(See p. 157 for answers)

1   The largest known swarm of locusts covered an area of:
    a) 400 sq yd b) 400 sq km c) 400 sq mi

2   Doménikos Theotokopoulos is better known as: a) Zorba
    the Greek b) Demis Roussos c) El Greco

3   In 1991 in the UK smoking-related diseases killed: a)
    13,000 b) 113,000 c) 213,000

4   A merino is: a) a Spanish sailor b) an Italian sculptor c) an
    Australian sheep

5   Wykehamists are old pupils of: a) Rugby School
    b) Marlborough College c) Winchester College

6   The poet laureate receives a yearly stipend of: a) £70
    b) £700 c) £7,000

7   In which equestrian sport is a 'sulky' an essential piece of
    equipment? a) dressage b) harness racing c) polo

8   The actor Richard Burton's real Welsh surname was:
    a) Jenkins b) Jones c) Davies

9   Which English city did the Romans call Eboracum?
    a) Chester b) Bath c) York

10 The area of Russia is so large that the UK would fit into it:
    a) 40 times b) 70 times c) 100 times

(See p. 158 for answers)

1   Which quantity has direction as well as magnitude?

2   Which physicist's law states that equal volumes of all gases, measured at the same temperature and pressure, contain the same number of molecules?

3   What describes a substance that exists in more than one form, differing in physical rather than chemical properties?

4   What is the ability of fluids to offer resistance to flow?

5   What is studied in the science of cryogenics?

6   Whose 'unified field theory' tried to explain the four fundamental forces in terms of a single, unified force?

7   What is the SI unit of magnetic flux density, named after a Croatian electrical engineer?

8   What was invented by Dennis Gabor in 1947, winning him a Nobel prize in 1971?

9   What does the acronym maser stand for?

10   What is described as an ionized gas with approximately equal numbers of positive and negative charges?

(See p. 158 for answers)

1 Who collaborated with Elvis Costello on his recording of 'Back on my Feet', and with Michael Jackson on 'Say, Say, Say'?

2 What was the title of Brecht's adaptation of *The Beggar's Opera*, which included the song 'Mac the Knife'?

3 Who founded Motown Records?

4 What is the better-known name of the drummer Richard Starkey?

5 Which jazz trumpeter is said to have invented bebop?

6 Who created the character of Ziggy Stardust in his glam-rock period of the 1970s?

7 Which coarse-voiced Texan was the lead singer with the San Francisco group Big Brother and the Holding Company?

8 What is the specialist instrument of Wynton Marsalis, the jazz musician?

9 What is the name for a record label that is completely separate from the large conglomerate companies?

10 What is the syncopated music in 2/4 time, usually played on the piano?

(See p. 159 for answers)

British Geography

1 What is the county town of County Antrim?

2 Which Scottish waterway links the North Sea with the Atlantic Ocean?

3 Which strait separates Anglesey from the mainland?

4 Which Home County was absorbed into Greater London in the 1974 reorganization?

5 What is the common igneous rock that forms Fingal's Cave and Giant's Causeway?

6 What is the name of the bight where the River Mersey joins the Irish Sea?

7 Which new town in Berkshire is home to the Meteorological Office?

8 Which English county contains the area called the Dukeries?

9 The names of which two English towns, one in the heart of England and one in Kent, are prefixed by the word 'Royal'?

10 What is the name of the national park where the highest point is Kinder Scout?

(See p. 159 for answers)

1   What is the name for the science of space travel?

2   What was first patented in 1846, and then manufactured by John Dunlop in 1888, for use on cars and bicycles?

3   Which shallow-drafted sailing vessel's name is derived from the Tamil for 'tied log'?

4   Which American space shuttle was built to replace *Challenger*?

5   In which part of an internal combustion engine is petrol mixed with air for feeding to the cylinders?

6   What is 31 miles long and runs from Folkestone to Sangatte?

7   Which early 20th-century car had the nickname Tin Lizzie?

8   What was the name of the jet-propelled car driven by Richard Noble, which set the world land-speed record at 633.5 mph?

9   Which was the first jet airliner to enter service in 1949?

10 Which vehicle has design variations known as open plenum, peripheral jet or flexible skirt?

(See p. 160 for answers)

1 Who was William IV's queen, after whom an Australian city was named?

2 What is the collective name for the three Low Countries of Europe?

3 What was the code of gallantry and honour that medieval knights were pledged to observe?

4 Which German educationist first opened 'kindergartens' where children learned through play?

5 Which European country has been ruled by Harald V since 1991?

6 Which were the two factions of the Russian Social Democratic Party whose names were taken from the words for 'majority' and 'minority'?

7 Which countries provide the five permanent members of the United Nations Security Council?

8 Who is the patron saint of music?

9 Which principality will become part of France if the reigning Prince dies without producing a male heir?

10 Which day of the week is named after the wife of the Norse god Odin?

(See p. 160 for answers)

ANSWERS

1	Balaclava helmet (Balaclava)
2	1666 (MDCLXVI) (Roman numerals)
3	The Tomb of the Unknown Soldier (Arlington; Unknown Soldier)
4	Rubik (Rubik)
5	Alphabet (alphabet)
6	Five years (United Nations)
7	Alexander (Alexander)
8	Desmond Tutu (Tutu – caption)
9	Frisbee (Frisbee)
10	Credit cards (credit card)

1	Rainforest (rainforest)
2	USA (USA – panel)
3	The Ecology Party (Green Party)
4	Fossil fuel (fossil fuel)
5	Friends of the Earth (Friends of the Earth)
6	Endangered species (CITES)
7	Ozone (ozone)
8	Chernobyl (Chernobyl; nuclear reactor; Ukraine – panel)
9	Green belt (green belt)
10	Unleaded petrol (unleaded petrol)

1   True (nightshade; potato; tomato)
2   False (Basie)
3   True (nicotine)
4   True (Antarctica)
5   True (Philip)
6   True (Prince)
7   False (Alaska)
8   False (calendar; year)
9   True (Caligula)
10 False (beaver)

1   Volley (badminton; table tennis)
2   At a rodeo (rodeo)
3   Boris Becker (Becker)
4   Muhammad Ali/Cassius Clay (Ali)
5   Brown (snooker)
6   Caber (caber, tossing the)
7   Three-day eventing/eventing (equestrianism)
8   Sky-diving (free falling)
9   Barcelona (Olympic venues)
10 Freestyle/crawl (swimming)

1	Africa (Africa)
2	Budapest (Budapest)
3	Anticyclone (anticyclone)
4	Amazon (Amazon)
5	Ecuador (Ecuador – panel)
6	Niagara River (Niagara Falls)
7	Canada (Canada – panel)
8	Hungary (Hungary – panel)
9	Anchorage (Alaska; Anchorage)
10	Equator (great circle; latitude and longitude)

1	a) black (bear)
2	b) Albania (Teresa)
3	a) 6 (prime ministers of Britain – panel)
4	c) Alaska (Alaska)
5	c) 8 stone (capybara)
6	b) gnomon (sun dial)
7	c) 16,000 ft (Antarctica)
8	b) Literature (Churchill)
9	c) the dong (Vietnam – panel)
10	a) right arm/right eye (Nelson)

1   Victoria and Albert (Albert; Victoria)
2   Hadrian's Wall (Hadrian; Hadrian's Wall)
3   Domesday Book (archive; Domesday Book)
4   Excommunicate (excommunication; Pius V)
5   The Great Plague (plague)
6   Christopher Columbus (Columbus)
7   England and Scotland (England: history; Scotland: history; Union, Act of)
8   American Civil War (Civil War, American)
9   Hardy (Hardy, Thomas Masterman)
10   The Crimean War (Crimean War; Nightingale)

1   Penguins (penguins)
2   Tadpole (amphibian)
3   Flamingo (flamingo)
4   Alligator (alligator)
5   Owl (owl)
6   Crab (crab)
7   Blue whale (whale)
8   Plankton (plankton)
9   Roadrunner (roadrunner: text and caption)
10   Migration (migration)

1 Neil Armstrong (Armstrong, Neil)
2 Assisi (Assisi)
3 Billionaire (billion)
4 Guy Fawkes (Fawkes; Gunpowder Plot)
5 Gordonstoun School (Gordonstoun)
6 The Adventure of Pinocchio (Collodi; Pinocchio)
7 Gypsies (Gypsy; Romany)
8 Interpol (Interpol)
9 Coroner (coroner)
10 Alibi (alibi)

1 Arkansas (United States of America – states panel)
2 General Norman Schwarzkopf (Schwarzkopf, Norman)
3 The American Constitution (constitution)
4 Muhammad Ali/Cassius Clay (Ali)
5 Judy Garland (Garland)
6 Gambling (Atlantic City; Las Vegas; Nevada)
7 Ronald Reagan (Reagan)
8 Wyoming (United States of America – states panel)
9 Glenn Miller (Miller, Glenn)
10 Memphis (Memphis)

1 Blackpool (Blackpool)
2 Avon (Avon)
3 Sherwood Forest (Nottinghamshire; Sherwood Forest)
4 Cumbria (Cumbria; Scafell Pike; Windermere)
5 Greenwich (Greenwich; Greenwich Mean Time)
6 M6 (motorway)
7 Ireland (Giant's Causeway; Macgillycuddy's Reeks)
8 Wales (Wales)
9 The Pennines (Pennines)
10 Aviemore (Aviemore; Cairngorms)

1 John (John, St; The Bible – panel)
2 Lazarus (Lazarus)
3 Aaron (Aaron)
4 Revelation (Revelation)
5 Proverbs (Proverbs)
6 Genesis (Genesis)
7 Jericho (Jericho; Joshua)
8 Judas Iscariot (Judas Iscariot)
9 Psalms (psalm)
10 Adam (Adam)

1	Alfred Hitchcock (Hitchcock)
2	Austrian (Schwarzenegger)
3	Steven Spielberg (Spielberg)
4	Dustin Hoffman (Hoffman, Dustin)
5	Roger Rabbit (Hoskins)
6	James Bond (Connery; Fleming, Ian; Moore, Roger)
7	Hepburn (Hepburn, Audrey and Katharine)
8	It was the first talking picture (Jolson)
9	Sylvester Stallone (Stallone)
10	Snow White and the Seven Dwarfs (Disney)

1	*Moby-Dick* (*Moby-Dick*)
2	Agatha Christie (Christie, Agatha)
3	Kenneth Grahame (Grahame)
4	Dr Watson (Holmes, Sherlock)
5	Mark Twain (Twain)
6	Sancho Panza (*Don Quixote de la Mancha*)
7	The Hobbits (Tolkien)
8	The Brontë family (Brontë)
9	Charles Dickens (Dickens)
10	Dracula (Dracula)

1 False (Amazon)
2 True (dinosaur)
3 True (Richard I *the Lionheart*)
4 True (Olympic Games)
5 False (CIA; CID)
6 True (The Bible)
7 False (Big Ben)
8 False (kilobyte)
9 True (dogfish)
10 True (dingo)

1 Alloys (alloy; amalgam; pewter; solder; steel)
2 Arithmetic (arithmetic)
3 Hypotenuse (Pythagoras; Pythagoras' theorem)
4 Holography (holography)
5 Computer Science (computer)
6 Heredity/inheritance (genetics; heredity)
7 Angles (angle)
8 Hydrogen (hydrogen)
9 Dynamite (Nobel Prize)
10 Hardware (hardware)

1. Additives (additive)
2. Cognac (cognac)
3. Chewing gum/bubble gum (chewing gum; chicle)
4. Sturgeon (caviar; sturgeon)
5. Roughage (fibre, dietary)
6. Haggis (haggis)
7. Aubergine (aubergine)
8. Avocado (avocado)
9. Beaujolais *nouveau* (Beaujolais)
10. Pancakes (Shrove Tuesday)

1. Batman (Batman)
2. James Herriot (Herriot, James)
3. Barry Humphries (Humphries)
4. Pantomime (pantomime)
5. Gospel (gospel music)
6. Jeeves and Wooster (Wodehouse)
7. Julie Andrews (Andrews, Julie)
8. Roald Dahl (Dahl, Roald)
9. The Muppets (Henson)
10. Cats (Eliot; Lloyd Webber)

1	Litmus (litmus)
2	Methane (methane)
3	Alcohol (alcoholic liquor)
4	Solid, liquid and gas (states of matter)
5	Gypsum (gypsum)
6	Fermentation (fermentation)
7	Chlorine (chlorine)
8	Gunpowder (gunpowder)
9	Diamond (diamond)
10	Salt (salt, common; sodium chloride)

1	Wisdom teeth (tooth)
2	37°C / 98.4°F (human body)
3	Heart (heart – caption)
4	Insulin (insulin; pancreas)
5	Jugular veins (jugular vein)
6	Feet (human body)
7	Brain (brain)
8	Hiccups (hiccup)
9	Capillaries (capillary)
10	Water (water)

1   Dick Turpin (highwayman; Turpin)
2   Hacking (hacking)
3   Military intelligence (intelligence)
4   Iron Curtain (Iron Curtain)
5   April Fool's Day/1 April (April Fool's Day)
6   Bedouins (Bedouin)
7   Tower of London (Tower of London)
8   Cruft (Cruft)
9   Charter (Atlantic Charter; Citizen's Charter; People's Charter)
10 Denier (denier)

1   Neil Kinnock (Kinnock – caption)
2   House of Commons (Commons, House of)
3   Douglas Hurd (Hurd)
4   Shadow Cabinet (Shadow Cabinet)
5   European Parliament (European Parliament)
6   James Callaghan (prime ministers of Britain – panel)
7   *Hansard* (*Hansard*)
8   Paddy Ashdown (Ashdown)
9   Three (act of Parliament)
10 Poll tax/community charge (poll tax)

1   Camelot (Camelot)
2   Labyrinth (Labyrinth)
3   Osiris (Egyptian religion; Isis; Osiris)
4   Gorgons (Gorgon)
5   Midas (Midas)
6   Narcissus (Echo; Narcissus)
7   Olympus (Olympus)
8   In Valhalla, in Norse myth (Valhalla)
9   Centaur (Sagittarius)
10 Odysseus (*Odyssey*; Penelope; Telemachus)

1   Pianoforte (piano)
2   Operas (Milan; Covent Garden)
3   The Proms/Promenade Concerts (promenade concert)
4   Gilbert and Sullivan (Gilbert; Sullivan)
5   Hungarian (Bartok; Kodaly; Liszt)
6   Harmonica (harmonica)
7   It wasn't discovered until 1930 (Holst; Pluto)
8   Concert harp (harp)
9   Mozart (Mozart)
10 Harmonium (harmonium)

1 Apollo 11 (Apollo project)
2 The *Titanic* (*Titanic*)
3 Concorde (Concorde; fligh – text and chronology)
4 Heavy goods vehicle (HGV)
5 Underground/the tube (underground)
6 Unmanned (Gagarin)
7 Helicopter (helicopter)
8 Train (railway – text and chronology)
9 Jumbo/jumbo jet (flight – chronology; jumbo jet)
10 Moped (motorcycle)

1 c) embellished waterspouts (gargoyles)
2 b) Hanover (Hanover; Saxe-Coburg-Gotha; Windsor)
3 b) half-man/half-horse (centaur)
4 b) $74^1/_2$ miles (United Kingdom – panel)
5 c) 1,763 days (Waite)
6 b) Eva Peron (Lloyd Webber; Peron)
7 a) Henry James (James, Henry)
8 c) Greg Norman (Norman, Greg)
9 b) 40 million (Jackson, Michael)
10 b) 30 ft (alimentary canal)

1   Sikhism (Sikhism)
2   Easter (Lent; Shrove Tuesday; Whit Sunday)
3   Islam (Islam)
4   Judaism (Judaism)
5   Buddhism (Buddhism)
6   Adventists (Adventists)
7   Hinduism (Hinduism)
8   Presbyterianism (Presbyterianism)
9   Quakers/Society of Friends (Friends, Society of)
10   Nirvana (Buddhism; nirvana)

1   Vinci (Leonardo)
2   Christopher Wren (St Paul's Cathedral)
3   Henry Moore (Moore, Henry)
4   Gauguin (Gauguin)
5   Lions (Landseer)
6   The Louvre (Louvre – caption; Pei)
7   Pieter Brueghel the Elder (Brueghel)
8   Norman/Romanesque (Norman architecture; Romanesque)
9   The Sydney Opera House (Sydney – caption)
10   L S Lowry (Lowry)

1 Eiffel Tower (Eiffel Tower)
2 Bar code (bar code)
3 National curriculum (national curriculum)
4 Pompeii (Herculaneum; Pompeii)
5 Greece (Greece – panel)
6 Edinburgh (Philip)
7 Capital punishment/hanging (capital punishment)
8 Ejector seat (ejector seat)
9 ECU (ECU)
10 Hans Christian Andersen (Andersen)

1 Archimedes Principle (Archimedes)
2 Decibel (decibel)
3 Marie Curie (Curie)
4 Anders Celsius (Celsius)
5 Amplifier (amplifier)
6 Lens (lens)
7 Conductor (conductor)
8 Seven (spectrum)
9 Calorie (calorie)
10 Inertia (inertia)

1	Elvis Presley (Presley)
2	Elton John (John, Elton)
3	Buddy Holly (Holly)
4	The Rolling Stones (Rolling Stones)
5	Bananarama (Bananarama)
6	Phil Collins (Collins, Phil)
7	Bob Geldof (Geldof)
8	Tina Turner (Turner, Tina)
9	Graceland (Simon, Paul)
10	Cliff Richard (Richard)

1	Alternative medicine (medicine, alternative)
2	Blood (blood groups)
3	Acquired immune deficiency syndrome (AIDS)
4	Tuberculosis (tuberculosis)
5	Fluoride (fluoride)
6	Ear, nose and throat (ENT)
7	Hepatitis (hepatitis)
8	Eyes (astigmatism; cataract; myopia; presbyopia)
9	Asthma (asthma)
10	Anaemia (anaemia)

1   Year (year)
2   Halley's comet (Halley's comet)
3   Pluto (planets – panel)
4   Craters (Moon)
5   Eclipse (eclipse)
6   Light year (light year)
7   The Southern Cross (Australia – panel; Crux)
8   Mercury and Venus (moon)
9   Black hole (black hole; quasar)
10 The Plough (Plough)

1   False (beet)
2   False (Chopin)
3   True (Socrates)
4   False (Arctic; continent)
5   True (mushroom; toadstool)
6   True (swastika)
7   False (Treasury)
8   True (Antarctica)
9   True (arachnid; scorpion; spider)
10 False – he sealed it because he couldn't write (John, 1167–1216)

1   Cuba (Cuba – panel)
2   China (China – panel)
3   The Camargue (Camargue)
4   Amman (Amman; Jordan)
5   Turkey (Bosporus)
6   Nagasaki (atom bomb; Nagasaki)
7   Hawaii (Cook, James; Hawaii)
8   The Netherlands (Netherlands – panel)
9   Boroughs (London; New York)
10 River Danube (Danube)

1   Johnson (Johnson, Andrew; Johnson, Lyndon B)
2   Crazy Horse and Sitting Bull (Crazy Horse; Custer; Little Bighorn; Sitting Bull – caption)
3   Hoover Dam (Colorado river; Hoover Dam)
4   Impeachment (impeachment; Nixon)
5   J Paul Getty (Getty)
6   Prohibition (Prohibition)
7   President (Arthur, Chester Alan; Hayes; Polk; USA presidents and elections – panel)
8   Irangate (Irangate; North, Oliver; Poindexter)
9   Gerald Ford (USA presidents and elections – panel)
10 Secretary of State (State Department)

1   Sumo wrestling (sumo wrestling)
2   Polo (polo)
3   Wimbledon, US Open, Australian Championships, French Championships (tennis)
4   Harlem Globetrotters (basketball; Harlem Globetrotters)
5   Heptathlon (heptathlon)
6   The first six (motor racing)
7   Ascot (Ascot; horse racing)
8   Sydney (cricket)
9   Curling (curling)
10 Gridiron (football, American)

1   Abraham Lincoln (Lincoln)
2   The Commonwealth (commonwealth)
3   Russia (Romanov dynasty; Russian rulers – panel)
4   Battle of Bosworth (Bosworth; Roses, Wars of the)
5   Gauls (Gauls)
6   Catherine Parr (Parr)
7   Adolf Hitler (Hitler)
8   Czechoslovakia (Czechoslovakia)
9   Battle of Hastings (Hastings, Battle of)
10 Italy (Axis; Italy)

1 Grantham (Newton; Thatcher)
2 Huxley (Huxley, Aldous and Julian)
3 Earth (tellurium)
4 Isaac Newton (Galileo; Newton)
5 Tuberculosis (Bronte; Chopin; Keats)
6 Jodhpur (Jodhpur)
7 Because they were the seventh, eighth, ninth and tenth months of the Roman calendar (calendar)
8 Esperanto (Esperanto; Zamenhof)
9 Bradford (Bradford)
10 Marquess (peerage)

1 *The Merry Wives of Windsor* (Shakespeare: the plays – panel)
2 Booker Prize (Booker Prize – list)
3 Haiku (*haiku*)
4 *The Metamorphosis* (Kafka)
5 Victor Hugo (Hugo)
6 *Gulliver's Travels* (*Gulliver's Travels*; Swift)
7 Hughes (Hughes, Thomas and Ted)
8 Hiawatha (*Hiawatha*; Longfellow)
9 *Nineteen Eighty-Four* (*Nineteen Eighty-Four*; Orwell)
10 Percy Bysshe Shelley (Shelley, Mary)

1   *Prince Igor* (Borodin)
2   Glyndebourne (Glyndebourne)
3   Scales (scale)
4   George I (Handel)
5   A violin bow (orchestra)
6   (Classical) guitar (Bream; guitar; Segovia)
7   Operas by Benjamin Britten (Britten)
8   James Galway (Galway)
9   *Fidelio* (Beethoven)
10 The 'New World' symphony (Dvořák)

1   c) Kirk Douglas (Douglas, Kirk)
2   a) Italy (Charles Edward Stuart)
3   a) Indonesia (Indonesia – panel)
4   a) Derbyshire (Derbyshire)
5   c) 15,000,000°C (Sun)
6   a) 1,293 ft (Dead Sea)
7   c) a train (railway; Shinkansen)
8   b) 130 (flea)
9   c) 200 mph (hurricane)
10 a) Catalan (Andorra – panel)

1   Amnion; amniotic membrane (amnion)
2   Retina (eye – caption; retina)
3   Synovial fluid (joint; synovial fluid)
4   The pulmonary vein (vein)
5   Pelvic girdle (pelvis)
6   Liver (liver)
7   Hormones (hormone; endocrine gland)
8   Ear drum (ear)
9   Haemoglobin (haemoglobin)
10 Lymph (lymph)

1   Mickey Mouse (Disney)
2   Ginger Rogers and Fred Astaire (Astaire; Rogers, Ginger)
3   Jodie Foster (Foster, Jodie)
4   Stan Laurel (Laurel and Hardy)
5   Marlon Brando (Brando)
6   Martin Scorsese (Scorsese)
7   Akira Kurosawa (Kurosawa)
8   Spaghetti Western (Eastwood)
9   John Wayne (Wayne – caption)
10 Arthur C Clarke (Clarke, Arthur C)

1   Gravity; electromagnetic force; strong nuclear force; weak
    nuclear force (electromagnetic force; forces, fundamental;
    gravity; strong nuclear force; weak nuclear force)
2   Kinetics (kinetics)
3   Family (family; genus)
4   Helix (helix)
5   Magnitude (magnitude; Richter Scale)
6   Sulphuric acid (sulphuric acid; vitriol)
7   On non-stick pans (polytetrafluoroethene)
8   Square (rhombus)
9   Relative humidity (humidity; hygrometer)
10 Bearing (bearing)

1   Crescent moon (crescent; Pakistan – panel; Tunisia – panel;
    Turkey – panel)
2   Elsinore (Helsinger)
3   Graffiti (graffiti)
4   Macao (Macao)
5   Jeremy (Ashdown)
6   Denim (Nîmes)
7   British Standards Institute (British Standards Institute)
8   Jordan (Jordan – panel)
9   A jewelled egg (Fabergé)
10 Canada (Commonwealth, British – panel)

1	Joni Mitchell (Mitchell, Joni)
2	Paul Hewson (U2)
3	Bruce Springsteen (Springsteen)
4	The Jackson Five (Jackson, Michael)
5	Mark Knopfler (Dire Straits)
6	Tim Rice (Lloyd Webber)
7	Tin Machine (Bowie – caption)
8	Country and western/country music (country and western)
9	Irving Berlin (Berlin, Irving)
10	The Who (Who, the)

1	Mediterranean Sea (Mediterranean Sea)
2	Carbon dioxide; methane; chlorofluorocarbons (greenhouse effect)
3	(Tropical) rainforest (rainforest)
4	*Rainbow Warrior* (Greenpeace)
5	Hedges/hedgerows (hedge)
6	Myxomatosis (myxomatosis)
7	Jonathon Porritt (Porritt)
8	Sweden (nuclear reactor)
9	Aral Sea (Aral Sea)
10	Sellafield (nuclear energy – caption; Sellafield)

1 False (Hadrian)
2 True (Netherlands, the)
3 True (snail)
4 True (human body)
5 True (football, Australian Rules)
6 True (mudskipper)
7 False (parliament)
8 True (Wodehouse)
9 True (smokers)
10 False (Mount Rushmore)

1 Sebastian Coe (Coe)
2 1969 (parliamentary reform – panel)
3 Edward Heath (Heath)
4 Federalism (Maastricht Summit)
5 The Citizen's Charter (Citizen's Charter)
6 Hugh Gaitskell (Gaitskell)
7 Speaker (Speaker)
8 Glenda Jackson (Jackson, Glenda)
9 Deselection (deselection)
10 Ombudsman (ombudsman)

1   Angelica (angelica)
2   Brine (brine)
3   Irradiation (food irradiation)
4   Lager (beer)
5   Ultra heat treated (food technology)
6   Roquefort (Roquefort)
7   Rice (rice)
8   Olives (olive)
9   Pasteurization (pasteurization)
10   Juniper (gin; juniper)

1   Ant (ant)
2   Appendix (appendix; vestigial organ)
3   Kangaroos (kangaroo)
4   Froghopper/spittlebug (froghopper)
5   Hummingbirds (hummingbird)
6   Squirrel (squirrel)
7   Cellulose (cellulose)
8   Koala (koala – caption)
9   Fungi (fungus)
10   Kelp (kelp; seaweed)

1 Caernarvon (Caernarvon)
2 Horatio (Kitchener; Nelson)
3 Haiti (Haiti – panel)
4 Napoleon Bonaparte (Napoleon I)
5 1931 (Commonwealth, British – panel)
6 Rasputin (Rasputin)
7 Chicago (Chicago)
8 Blenheim Palace (Churchill)
9 Tog (tog)
10 The press (Fourth Estate)

1 Paul Klee (Klee)
2 Frank Lloyd Wright (Wright, Frank Lloyd)
3 The Sistine Chapel ceiling (Michelangelo; Sistine Chapel)
4 Gothic (Gothic architecture)
5 Impressionists (Impressionism)
6 Toulouse-Lautrec (Toulouse-Lautrec)
7 George Stubbs (Stubbs)
8 Baroque (Baroque)
9 Guernica (Picasso)
10 Jackson Pollock (Pollock)

1   Arsenic (arsenic)
2   Tin (bronze; pewter)
3   Mohs Scale (Mohs Scale)
4   Iodine (iodine)
5   Radioactive (transuranic element)
6   Dry ice (dry ice)
7   Sublimation (sublimation)
8   Iron (hematite; iron; limonite; magnetite)
9   Halogens (halogen; Periodic Table)
10   Verdigris (verdigris)

1   Isadora Duncan (Duncan)
2   Phineas T Barnum (Barnum)
3   Ballet (ballet)
4   Montreux (Montreux)
5   Peter Cook (Cook)
6   Bruce Lee (Lee, Bruce)
7   Stephen Sondheim (Sondheim)
8   The Old Vic (Old Vic)
9   Dennis Potter (Potter)
10   Warren Beatty (MacLaine)

1   b) 1908 (Canberra)
2   b) karate (karate)
3   b) 90,000,000 (Earth)
4   c) King Zog (Albania; Zog)
5   c) 206 bones (human body)
6   b) 6,500,000 (underground)
7   b) 969 (Methuselah)
8   c) football (football, association)
9   a) Turkey (Ararat; Turkey – panel)
10 c) her maid (Macdonald)

1   The Potteries (Potteries, the)
2   Holyhead (Anglesey; Holyhead)
3   Lough Neagh (Neagh, Lough)
4   Sheffield (Sheffield)
5   Isle of Wight (Wight, Isle of)
6   Cheviots (Cheviots)
7   Birmingham (Birmingham)
8   Watling Street (Watling Street)
9   Greenwich Meridian (latitude and longitude; time)
10 Cairngorms (Aviemore; Cairngorms)

1	Nymphs (nymphs)
2	Hope (Pandora)
3	River Styx (Styx)
4	Seals/dugongs (mermaid)
5	Cassandra (Cassandra)
6	Tintagel (Arthur; Tintagel)
7	The Lorelei (Lorelei)
8	Ambrosia (ambrosia)
9	He was not to look back at her as he led her out of Hades (Orpheus)
10	Balder (Balder)

1	Equilibrium (equilibrium)
2	Speed of light (energy)
3	Frequency (frequency)
4	Inductance (henry; inductance)
5	Standard temperature and pressure (NTP; STP)
6	Diode (diode)
7	Momentum (momentum)
8	Friction (friction)
9	Solenoid (solenoid)
10	Ultrasonics (ultrasonics; ultrasound)

1 Bridges (bridge)
2 Mounties (Mounties; Royal Canadian Mounted Police)
3 Cancer (cancer; crab)
4 Cartel (cartel)
5 Kazakhstan (Kazakhstan – panel)
6 Colombia (Colombia – panel; Medellín)
7 Longleat (Wiltshire)
8 Anticoagulants (anticoagulant)
9 Pecan (hickory)
10 Pope Gregory (Gregory XIII)

1 The Ten Commandments (Decalogue)
2 Frankincense and myrrh (frankincense; myrrh)
3 Shem; Ham; Japheth (Noah)
4 John's Gospel (gospel)
5 David (David; Solomon)
6 Mammon (Mammon)
7 Matthew (Matthew)
8 Genesis; Exodus; Leviticus; Numbers; Deuteronomy (The Bible – panel)
9 The Evangelists (evangelist)
10 Mary Magdalene (Mary Magdalene, St)

1	Saturn (planets – panel)
2	Earth (Earth)
3	Copernicus (astronomy; Copernicus)
4	The Sun (Sun)
5	Voyager I and II (Voyager probes)
6	Mercury (planet)
7	Nebulae (nebula)
8	Polaris (Polaris)
9	Parsec (parsec)
10	The Big Bang theory; the steady-state theory (Big Bang; steady-state theory; universe)

1	Orange (black box)
2	*Discovery* (*Discovery*)
3	Bicycle (bicycle)
4	Saturn V (rocket; Saturn rocket)
5	Rolls and Royce (Rolls; Royce)
6	Geostationary (geostationary orbit)
7	Amelia Earhart (Earhart)
8	Model-T Ford (Ford)
9	Kawasaki (Kawasaki; motorcycle)
10	Kerosene (kerosene)

1 Joseph Lister (Lister)
2 Lesion (lesion)
3 Lassa fever (Lassa fever)
4 Placebo (placebo)
5 Measles (measles)
6 Quinine (quinine)
7 Rhesus monkey (rhesus factor; rhesus)
8 Smallpox (smallpox)
9 Legionnaire's disease (legionnaire's disease)
10 Indigestion (dyspepsia)

1 Mormon (Mormon; Smith, Joseph)
2 Islam (Islam)
3 Lourdes (Bernadette, St)
4 Mardi Gras (Lent; Mardi Gras; Shrove Tuesday)
5 Dalai Lama (Dalai Lama)
6 Ecumenical movement (ecumenical movement)
7 Moonies (Moon; Moonie; Unification Church)
8 Muezzin (muezzin)
9 Jesuits (Jesuit; Ignatius Loyola, St)
10 Shinto (Shinto)

1 Rose Theatre (Globe Theatre; Rose Theatre)
2 Mafia (Mafia)
3 Descartes (Descartes)
4 Breton (Breton language)
5 Hebridean (Hebrides; Western Isles)
6 The Thames (Thames)
7 Geneva (Geneva)
8 GCE 'O' levels; CSE (GCE; GCSE)
9 Sir Christopher Wren (Wren)
10 Summit conference (summit conference)

1 Mariana Trench (Mariana Trench)
2 Mali (Mali – panel)
3 The Falkland Islands (Falkland Islands)
4 Genoa (Genoa)
5 The Levant (Levant)
6 Minnesota (Minnesota)
7 Murmansk (Murmansk)
8 Venezuela (Angel Falls; Venezuela – panel)
9 Moraine (moraine)
10 Australia (Canberra)

1   Maurits Escher (Escher)
2   Walter Gropius (Bauhaus; Gropius)
3   The Graces (Graces)
4   Edwin Lutyens (Lutyens)
5   Rembrandt (Rembrandt)
6   The Medici family (Uffizi)
7   Joshua Reynolds (Reynolds; Royal Academy of Arts)
8   Crystal Palace (Crystal Palace; Great Exhibition; Paxton)
9   Utrillo (Utrillo)
10 Francis Bacon (Bacon)

1   True (Memphis)
2   False (Constitution)
3   True (Robert I the Devil; William I the Conqueror)
4   True (Newton)
5   False (Orkneys, South)
6   False (marsupial; numbat)
7   False (railway – chronology; Stephenson, George)
8   True (inferno)
9   True (beaver; chipmunk; porcupine; rodent; squirrel)
10 False (Ivy League)

1   Scutari (Nightingale)
2   King Idris (Khaddhafi; Libya)
3   Pierre de Villeneuve (Nelson)
4   Gibraltar (Gibraltar; Spanish Succession, War of the)
5   Henrietta (Maria) (Charles I of Britain; Henrietta Maria)
6   Rosetta Stone (Rosetta Stone)
7   Richard Nixon (Nixon, Richard)
8   Stanley and Livingstone (Livingstone, David; Stanley, Henry Morton)
9   Joseph Stalin (Stalin)
10 Stephen (English sovereigns from 900 – panel; Henry I of England; Stephen)

1   *Under Milk Wood* (Thomas, Dylan)
2   Larousse (Larousse)
3   Cordelia (*King Lear*)
4   Robert Southey (Southey)
5   Blank verse (blank verse; Shakespeare)
6   John Milton (Milton)
7   Christopher Marlowe (Marlowe)
8   Walt Whitman (Whitman)
9   Angry Young Men (Angry Young Men)
10 Benjamin Disraeli (Disraeli)

1   Leaf (leaf – diagram)
2   Narwhal (narwhal)
3   Nacre (mother-of-pearl; pearl)
4   Oxalic acid (oxalic acid; rhubarb)
5   Reproduce (amoeba)
6   Latex (latex; rubber plant)
7   Kookaburra (kingfisher; kookaburra)
8   Hydrophytes (hydrophyte)
9   Aestivation (aestivation)
10 Beaver (beaver)

1   Fringe theatre (fringe theatre)
2   Gummo (Marx Brothers)
3   Kabuki (Kabuki)
4   Kenneth Branagh (Branagh)
5   George and Ira Gershwin (Gershwin)
6   L Frank Baum (Wizard of Oz, The Wonderful)
7   Maurice Chevalier (Chevalier)
8   Sir Harry Lauder (Lauder)
9   Benny Goodman (Goodman, Benny)
10 Estragon and Vladimir (Beckett – quote)

1	Information technology (information technology)
2	Inkatha movement (Buthelezi; Inkatha)
3	25 March (calendar)
4	Grimaldi (Monaco)
5	Westminster Abbey (Westminster Abbey)
6	Women (Salic law)
7	Tom (Morse code – diagram)
8	Ergonomics (ergonomics)
9	Koh-i-noor (Koh-i-noor)
10	Khalistan (Khalistan; Sikhism)

1	Sago (sago)
2	Plantain (banana; plantain)
3	Rye (rye)
4	Stilton (Stilton)
5	Nonalcoholic (alcohol; alcoholic liquor; ethanol)
6	Mace (nutmeg)
7	Sugar (sweetener)
8	Durum flour (flour; pasta)
9	Orchids (vanilla)
10	Saffron (saffron)

1. Dyscalculia (dyslexia)
2. Gout (gout)
3. Leprosy (leprosy)
4. Embolism (embolism)
5. Dopamine (dopamine; Parkinson's Disease)
6. Nitrogen (bends)
7. Menthol (menthol)
8. Lymphatic system (Hodgkin's disease)
9. Ligature (ligature)
10. Salk (Salk)

1. Paderewski (Paderewski)
2. Cremona (Amati; Cremona; Guarneri; Stradivari)
3. Messiaen (Messiaen)
4. Richard Wagner (Bayreuth; Wagner, Richard)
5. Faust (Berlioz; Busoni; Faust; Gounod)
6. Viol (viol)
7. Malcolm Williamson (Williamson, Malcolm)
8. Köchel (Mozart)
9. Haydn (Haydn)
10. Sir Henry Wood (promenade concert; Wood)

1	a) bats (banana)
2	c) Michael Caine (Caine)
3	a) 1860 (golf)
4	b) US judge (loganberry)
5	b) empty orchestra (karaoke)
6	a) pheasant (peacock)
7	a) two (Henry VIII of England)
8	c) 50,000 (nuclear warfare)
9	a) Italy (Italy – panel)
10	a) 800 million (bicycle)

1	Genetic fingerprinting (genetic fingerprinting; Jeffreys, Alec)
2	Bionics (bionics)
3	Mendeleyev (Mendeleyev; periodic table of the elements)
4	Alfred Wallace (Wallace, Alfred R)
5	Lichen (lichen; litmus)
6	Scalene (triangle)
7	Mega (mega-)
8	Computer (analytical engine; Babbage)
9	Pitchblende (pitchblende; uraninite; uranium)
10	Lavoisier (Lavoisier)

1   Croquet; polo (croquet; polo)
2   Scunthorpe United (Botham)
3   Braemar Gathering (Braemar; Highland Games)
4   American/National Football Conference (football, American)
5   Kayak, Canadian-style canoe (canoeing)
6   Cricket; Australian rules football (cricket; football, Australian rules)
7   Nine (baseball)
8   Rugby Union (Rugby Union)
9   100 m; 200 m; long jump; 4×100 m relay (Lewis, Carl; Owens)
10 Luge (toboggan)

1   Ilion (*Iliad*)
2   *Infanta* (*infante*)
3   Klondike river (Klondike)
4   Yakuza (*yakuza*)
5   Libra (Libra; zodiac)
6   A book (ISBN; library)
7   A pound coin (pound)
8   Romance languages (Romance languages)
9   Top the appropriate letter with a short horizontal bar – e.g. $\overline{V}$ is $5 \times 1,000 = 5,000$) (Roman numerals)
10 P L Travers (Mary Poppins)

1   Luke (Luke)
2   Aramaic (Aramaic language)
3   Elisabeth (Elisabeth)
4   New Testament (New Testament)
5   Philistine (Delilah)
6   Saul; David (Samuel)
7   Ruth (Ruth)
8   Deborah (Deborah)
9   Bishop of Ephesus (John, St)
10 Ruth; Esther (Bible – panel)

1   Prince William Sound (Alaska; oil spill; Prince William
      Sound)
2   Peat (peat)
3   Bangladesh (Bangladesh – panel; global warming; greenhouse
      effect)
4   Iceland (Iceland – panel)
5   Nepal (Nepal – panel)
6   Acid rain (acid rain; sulphur dioxide)
7   The Orkney Islands (Orkney Islands)
8   River Po (Italy – panel; Po)
9   Athens (Athens; Greece – panel)
10 Yellowstone National Park (national park; Yellowstone
      National Park)

1   New Mexico (New Mexico)
2   Warren Commission (Kennedy, John F; Warren, Earl)
3   Lake Michigan (Michigan, Lake; Great Lakes)
4   Ronald Reagan (Reagan)
5   The first ten amendments of the Constitution (Bill of Rights)
6   Berkeley (Berkeley)
7   Michael Collins (Apollo project)
8   London Bridge (Arizona)
9   The Manhattan Project (Manhattan Project)
10   President Andrew Johnson (impeachment; Johnson, Andrew)

1   False (pound)
2   True (Union of Soviet Socialist Republics – *abortive anti-Gorbachev coup*)
3   True (Sinclair, Clive)
4   False (harmattan; wind)
5   True (tartan)
6   True (Anubis)
7   True (salt, common)
8   True (wasp)
9   True (Scotland – history)
10   True (Tokyo)

1   Water (water)
2   Corundum (corundum)
3   Tungsten (tungsten)
4   Polyesters (polyesters)
5   Radon (radon)
6   Iridium (iridium)
7   Cinnabar (cinnabar; mercury)
8   Polyvinylchloride (PVC)
9   Titration (titration)
10   Benzene (benzene –caption)

1   Lord Chancellor (Chancellor, Lord; Speaker)
2   Treaties of Rome (Rome, Treaties of)
3   Gladstone (Gladstone)
4   John Major (Lamont; Major)
5   Chairman of the party (cabinet – panel)
6   David Steel (Liberal Party)
7   Poll tax (Peasants' Revolt)
8   1928 (parliament – panel)
9   Cornwall (Cornwall)
10   Secretary of state for the environment (Heseltine)

1   Adrian IV (Adrian IV)
2   Lilith (Lilith)
3   *Mahābhārata*; *Rāmāyana* (*Mahābhārata*; *Rāmāyana*)
4   Islam (Islam)
5   Canonization (canonization)
6   Archbishop of York (archbishop)
7   The Anointed One (Christ)
8   Baha'i (Baha'i)
9   Ramadan (Ramadan)
10   Taoism (Taoism)

1   Australia (wattle)
2   Sauna (sauna)
3   Ruskin (Ruskin)
4   Yggdrasil (Yggdrasil)
5   Vivienne Westwood and Malcolm McLaren (Westwood)
6   Bouvier (Kennedy, John)
7   Quango (quango)
8   *Mir* (*Mir*)
9   Robben Island (Robben Island)
10   Isle of Man (Man, Isle of)

1   Venus (Venus)
2   Galaxies (galaxy; Hubble)
3   Pluto (astronomy – chronology; Pluto)
4   Van Allen (radiation) belts (atmosphere; Van Allen radiation belts)
5   Parallax (parallax)
6   Orion (Betelgeuse; Orion)
7   Ceres (asteroid; Ceres)
8   Neptune (Neptune)
9   Andromeda (Andromeda)
10 Jupiter (planet)

1   Mary Pickford (Pickford)
2   Francis Ford Coppola (Coppola)
3   *Monsieur Verdoux* (Chaplin)
4   Randolph Hearst (Hearst)
5   Wolves (*Dances with Wolves*) (Academy Awards – panel)
6   Madonna (Madonna)
7   Sergei Eisenstein (Eisenstein)
8   Cary Grant (Grant – caption)
9   *Heaven's Gate* (Cimino; United Artists)
10 Faye Dunaway (Dunaway)

1   Spleen (lymphocyte; spleen)
2   Endorphins (endorphin)
3   Keloid (keloid)
4   Keratin (keratin)
5   Iris (iris)
6   Lactic acid (lactic acid)
7   Hammer; anvil; stirrup (malleus; incus; stapes) (ear)
8   Melanin (albinism; melanism)
9   Teeth (tooth)
10 Histamine (allergy; histamine)

1   Kali (Kali)
2   Amaterasu (Amaterasu)
3   Aegis (Aegis)
4   India (unicorn)
5   Pygmalion (Pygmalion)
6   The Fates (Fates)
7   Asgard (Asgard)
8   Nereids (nymph)
9   Kwannon/Kwanyin (Kwannon)
10 Elysium (Elysium)

1	c) 400 square miles (locust)
2	c) El Greco (Greco, El)
3	b) 113,000 (smoking)
4	c) an Australian sheep (merino)
5	c) Winchester College (Winchester)
6	a) £70 (poet laureate)
7	b) harness racing (horse racing)
8	a) Jenkins (Burton, Richard)
9	c) York (York)
10	b) 70 times (United Kingdom – panel; USSR – constituent republics 1992–91)

1	Vector quantity (vector quantity)
2	Amadeo Avogadro (Avogadro)
3	Allotropic (allotropy)
4	Viscosity (viscosity)
5	Very low temperatures (cryogenics)
6	Einstein (Einstein)
7	Tesla (tesla)
8	Holography/holograms (Gabor)
9	Microwave amplification by stimulated emission of radiation (maser)
10	Plasma (plasma)

1. Paul McCartney (McCartney)
2. The Threepenny Opera/Die Dreigroschenoper (Brecht)
3. Berry Gordy Jr (Motown)
4. Ringo Starr (Beatles, the)
5. Dizzie Gillespie (Gillespie)
6. David Bowie (Bowie)
7. Janis Joplin (Joplin, Janis)
8. Trumpet (jazz)
9. Indie/independent (indie)
10. Ragtime (ragtime)

1. Belfast (Antrim; Belfast)
2. Caledonian Canal (Caledonian Canal)
3. Menai Strait (Menai Strait)
4. Middlesex (Home Counties)
5. Basalt (basalt)
6. Liverpool Bay (Mersey)
7. Bracknell (Bracknell)
8. Nottinghamshire (Nottinghamshire)
9. Royal Leamington Spa; Royal Tunbridge Wells (Leamington; Tunbridge Wells, Royal)
10. The Peak District (Peak District)

1. Astronautics (astronautics)
2. The pneumatic tyre (Dunlop)
3. Catamaran (catamaran)
4. *Endeavor* (space shuttle)
5. Carburettor (car; carburation)
6. The Channel Tunnel (Channel Tunnel)
7. Model-T Ford (car – chronology)
8. *Thrust 2* (*Thrust 2*)
9. Comet (flight – chronology)
10. Hovercraft (hovercraft – caption)

1. Adelaide (Adelaide)
2. Benelux(Benelux; Low Countries)
3. Chivalry (chivalry)
4. Froebel (Froebel)
5. Norway (Norway – panel)
6. Bolshevik and Menshevik (Bolshevik; Menshevik)
7. UK; USA; Russia; China; France (United Nations Security Council – panel)
8. St Cecilia (Cecilia, St)
9. Monaco (Monaco)
10. Friday (Freya)